INFORMATION
AND THE
CRISIS ECONOMY

INFORMATION AND THE CRISIS ECONOMY

Herbert I. Schiller

University of California, San Diego

New York   Oxford
Oxford University Press
1986

Oxford University Press
Oxford New York Toronto
Delhi Bombay Calcutta Madras Karachi
Petaling Jaya Singapore Hong Kong Tokyo
Nairobi Dar es Salaam Capetown
Melbourne Auckland

and associated companies in
Beirut Berlin Ibadan Nicosia

First published in 1984 by Ablex Publishing Corporation, New Jersey

First issued in paperback in 1986 by Oxford University Press, Inc.
200 Madison Avenue, New York NY 10016

Oxford is a registered trademark of Oxford University Press

Library of Congress Cataloging-in-Publication Data

Schiller, Herbert I., 1919–
    Information and the crisis economy.

    Includes indexes.
    1. Telecommunication—Social aspects. 2. Computers
and civilization. 3. Mass Media—Social aspects.
4. Economic history—1971–   . 5. Political participation. I. Title.
HE7651.S34   1986   302.2'34   86-2374
ISBN 0-19-520514-6 (pbk.)

Some of the material in this book has appeared elsewhere in either earlier or slightly
different versions. I thank the editors and publishers of *The Columbia Journal of World
Business*; Longman, publisher of Jerry L. Salvaggio's *Telecommunications: Issues and
Choices for Society*; UNESCO's Division of the Free Flow of Information and
Communication Policies; Ablex Publishing Corporation, the publisher of Vincent Mosco's
and Janet Wasko's *The Critical Communications Review*, Vol. II; and *Information and
Behavior*, Volume 1, 1984.

Printing (last digit): 9 8 7 6 5 4 3 2 1

Printed in the United States of America

Contents

Acknowledgements

It was especially helpful to have Frank Webster as a colleague at the time I began this work. Our discussions were of immeasurable assistance to me. Leena Paldán took time from a busy schedule to read the manuscript during a one week visit I made to the University of Tampere. I thank her for her constructive comments. Eileen Mahoney, once more, gave me valuable criticism and encouragement. Kim Thompson typed the final draft of the manuscript under time constraints, and did a fine job.

I hope my colleagues and friends in Paris and at UNESCO will accept a general acknowledgement and expression of appreciation for the comfortable ambience they helped to create for me while I worked on this project during a six months' appointment at the University of Paris (VIII), in 1982–1983. All the same, I must mention Francois Xavier Hutin, Bernard Miege, Pierre Dommergues, Michele and Armand Mattelart, Patrice Flichy, Lisa and Sammi Dorra, Rosalind Behringer and Seth Siegelaub, Francois Mariet and Roque Faraone.

Mel Voigt provided advice and support throughout this undertaking. Dan and Zach Schiller, as they have done many times before, read the manuscript as it progressed and kept me aware of what I was about.

In the end, this work is the outcome of the ongoing dialogue with Anita, carried on daily, during our walks by the ocean and our nightly promenades through the vacant streets of La Jolla. Specifically, the chapter "Information and the Push for Privatization and Productivity in the Economy" must be regarded as a joint effort. No one has paid closer attention to and analyzed this development more thoroughly than Anita Schiller.

La Jolla
May, 1984

Introduction

Some may wonder why this work is titled *Information and the Crisis Economy*. After all, the President of the United States, as recently as January 1984, told the nation, "Before us stands the prospect of an extended era of peace, prosperity, growth with a rising standard of living for all Americans."[1] Besides, modest improvements have been registered over the lows of 1981–1982 and unemployment has dipped slightly (though it is still peaking in Europe).[2]

Recent short-term changes in industrial activity, however, can hardly conceal the massive economic and social instabilities that now exist, nationally and globally. The possibility that these may precipitate cataclysmic breakdowns, *at any time,* is the dominant feature of this era.

Though no one knows what the level of joblessness will be when the effects of automation and robotization are fully felt in the years ahead, the Western crisis goes beyond economic shutdown and unemployment. It is at the same time, a fearful armaments race, utilizing the most advanced high technologies, with the possibility of nuclear war a steadily increasing peril.

Leaving aside the economic resource distortions this vast consumption of material and labor power produces, it engenders a climate of fear and anxiety that permeates the social atmosphere and penetrates human relationships in ways unable to be fully apprehended and certainly not measurable.

The ballooning national deficit—the outcome of huge military spending without taxation, so that people will tolerate the outlay—is yet another ingredient of the crisis that may be in the making.

The crisis affects the less industrialized nations no less lightly. Mortgaged to more than an 800 billion dollar debt, the poorer countries face annual interest charges that often exceed the value of their total exports. The financial debacle waiting to materialize, inevitably will spill back into the already-industrialized states, as their mighty banking institutions confront massive defaults.

The crisis is ecological. It arises out of the gargantuan resource wastage, incident to a productive system with a global outreach, which relies on a relentless stimulation of consumer demand rather than on planned social use. The skyrocketing military expenditures compound the resource despoliation and depletion.

Finally, the disorders induced by the economic, political, and military policies designed to maintain imperial power, constitute a deepening overall social crisis. They affect directly the lives of tens of millions of people. Crime and the pervasive drug culture reveal the well-advanced state of social disarray in the nation.

The view from the outside is confirmatory. The Rector of the United Nations University in Tokyo, Dr. Soedjatmoko, a prominent Indonesian intellectual, describes the "Nature of the Global Crisis" in these terms:

> Today, the whole international system itself is in a state of crisis and the cohesions—political, economic, social and otherwise—which have held it together, are coming unstuck at an alarming rate.[3]

In international finance, "a three trillion Euro-Currency is virtually beyond control"; and, "nations stricken by hunger and poverty must pay as much as $125 billion a year on their debts." On the threat of war, "the world has lost political control over the nuclear arms race and the arms trade," and "a labor force of more than one-hundred million people are paid directly or indirectly by defense ministries..."

India's Prime Minister, Indira Gandhi, concurred with Soedjatmoko's assessment:

> I entirely agree that we cannot solve our economic and financial crisis within existing international structures. I go further and say that none of the present structures or even thought-processes are capable of providing satisfactory answers to the large crisis of our civilization.[3]

It is the contention of this work that the multiplying informational activities and the growing stock of instrumentation around us are attributable, in large part, to the economic, political, and cultural pressures and strains produced by the general crisis of the world market system.

Information and information technologies have been seized upon as the means to alleviate and overcome the crisis. At the same time, they confer greater authority and offer increased returns to information controllers and powerful users.

In sum, the aim in what follows is to examine some of the means by which the new information capabilities are being applied for the purpose of dealing with the generalized crisis, especially but not exclusively, in the United States.

As these developments are still in a relatively early stage, the full impacts are yet to be experienced. Yet one conclusion already is inescapable: Technological solutions devoid of social acountability will be terribly costly to millions of human beings.

Yet what is happening in the American economy is no laboratory experiment. An enormous technico-social transformation is underway. Great numbers of people already are, and still more will be, affected in the next few years. How individuals regard these changes in their own and their neighbors' lives and living environments is of crucial importance.

On these views and the popular mobilizations that could emerge from them will depend whether there will be efforts to introduce human values and social criteria into the technico-industrial decisions now being made throughout the economy. Failing this, a continued, if not accelerated, drive to make production more "efficient" may well obtain a respite and continued profitability for a few thousand transnational companies. It will produce, also, misery and desolation for those who will be the rejects of an inflexible and socially unconcerned dollars-and-cents calculus of productive efficiency.

Popular understanding about what is happening, therefore, is an urgent need. But how to achieve it? Information is being applied to the production side of the economy in a particular way, for private, corporate advantage. Yet, it is also being applied to the human side. Here it is used to make people accept and believe that current developments are benign, if not beneficial. It is applied to minimizing or deprecating opposition and to denying alternate options that might provide a more humane direction to the emerging information-based economy.

Thus, the push toward a corporate-controlled information society proceeds along a two-lane road. One lane is the economy itself. The other is popular consciousness. As movement quickens on the production lane, the road along which consciousness travels receives increasing attention as well.

Messages designed to persuade and to cajole the people into believing that information technology holds the key to general improvement saturate the media, receive corporate support,[4] are echoed in University courses and conferences,[5] and account for a considerable chunk of the governmental informational effort.[6]

All these efforts notwithstanding, popular acquiescence cannot be taken for granted. In fact, it is the recognition that there is skepticism and wariness, in difficult to specify levels, that accounts for the barrage being laid down.

Caught up as they are, and increasingly will be, in crises that put them either out of work or in stress-filled jobs, or drafted for overseas interventions or domestic "law and order" programs, bombarded with "happy media" while daily existence grows more uncertain and anxious, what may be expected from the American people?

At no time in recent history has the prospect for a decent life for people everywhere seemed more threatened. In the United States, there has been an almost continuous weakening of the democratic order over a four-decade interval. It is not, of course, an uninterrupted decline. Rather it is a progressive yielding of position to the money power in the governing mechanisms of the economy. It is the outcome of the near-complete capture of the national economic, political, and cultural machinery by corporate wealth and power.

The results are evident on all sides and are reviewed in the following chapters. But if one overarching generalization can be made, it is that there is now an almost complete absence of alternative visions for the people and for the economy, unless more of the same can be understood as a vision.

The penetration of corporate power and corporate thinking is now so extensive that the calculus of business performance has become the almost automatic measurement of individual purpose and achievement.

To what extent a social perspective can regain prominence in the politics and the consciousness of Americans is the transcendent question. The answer depends greatly on the character of the information available to the people. What follows, therefore, is an analysis of the determinants of the information supply now being provided, and, unless there is a major reversal, what may be expected to be delivered in the future.

NOTES TO THE INTRODUCTION

1. Leonard Silk, "Economy's One Bad Sign Still Dominates the News," The *New York Times,* February 5, 1984.

2. The *New York Times,* January 27, 1984.

3. Soedjatmoko, "Non-Alignment and Beyond," 16th Jawaharlal Nehru Memorial Lecture, November 13, 1982, *The Non-Aligned World,* New Delhi, Vol. 1, No. 1, January–March, 1983, pp. 5–21.

4. A new Information Age Institute, proposed by the Computer and Business Equipment Manufacturers Association (CBEMA), for example, is designed, the *Chronicle of International Information* reports, "to accelerate and *depoliticize* American passage into the post-industrial society." "Taking on Technophobia," *Chronicle of International Communication,* December 1983, Vol. IV, No. 10, p. 6 (emphasis added).

5. One example, among many, of the interlocking interests of academic, government, and the corporate world in promoting the positive features of the new information technologies, was a lecture series offered at the University of Southern California's Annenberg School of Communication in 1983–1984. Promisingly titled "The Computer Culture," the announcement states the lectures are "funded by a grant from ITT" and that the "speakers will uncover the creative forces that are shaping computers and the impacts these systems are having." *The Annenberg Record,* University of Southern California, 1984/1, p. 8.

6.   At the end of more than a month-long jaunt across American in 1983, financed by the United States Information Agency and the United States Telecommunications Training Institute, a group of foreign visitors with "senior positions" in the information field in their own countries came together at an Aspen Institute facility in Maryland, the Wye plantation—an especially appropriately named meeting place for ex-colonials.

There, participants from several Third World states and others from Europe and North America considered "International Issues in Communication Technology and Policy." This particular event was organized by the Academy for Educational Development, a U.S.-financed research enterprise in the field of education. The seminar received additional financial support from the Benton Foundation and the Communications Satellite Corporation (Comsat). "International Issues in Communication and Technology and Policy," Academy for Educational Development, Washington, D.C., 1983.

More systematically still, the Presidentially appointed United States Advisory Commission on Public Diplomacy, chaired by the President of the ultra-conservative Heritage Foundation, in its 1983 Annual Report recommended widely stepped up research and development on direct satellite broadcasting (DBS) technology, to enable Made-in-America messages to reach global audiences *directly,* circumventing local and national sovereignty around the world. 1983 Report of the United States Advisory Commission on Public Diplomacy to the President of the United States, Washington, D.C., 1983.

Chapter One

The New Information Technologies Combat the Western Economic Crisis

World war, social revolution, and economic crisis are the dominant phenomena of this century. No other events compare with the First and Second World Wars, the big depression of the late 1920s and 1930s, the great Russian and Chinese Revolutions, and the rise of a global anti-imperialist movement shattering the old European colonial empires in the post-World War II years.

Still, for thirty years the economic malaise affecting the center of the world business system was obscured by the rebuilding and general expansion in Western Europe, Japan, and North America after World War II. The massive unemployment in the United States that disappeared only with the outbreak of war in 1939 was conveniently forgotten. In the postwar period, along with other expressions of (misplaced) confidence, there was a boomlet in studies that announced the end of political struggles and the capability of private enterprise to provide a viable economic order.

Some of this has changed in the last few years. Instead of the end of economic malfunctioning, problems pop up on every side: inflation, stagflation, plant closings, regional decay, social decay. Most troubling of all, unemployment, regarded as a minor nuisance in the 1950s and 1960s, and not expected to exceed four percent of the labor force at its worst, is back at, or near, double digit levels. The allowable limits—who sets these boundaries?—have been extended to six and, more recently, to eight percent of the working force. In the United Kingdom, where the crisis is of almost disaster proportions, unemployment tolerances have moved from one percent (1945 perspective) to close to fifteen percent today.

A report to the Club of Rome in 1982 gloomily noted: "that we may be entering a long period of considerable and probably endemic unemployment..." (p. 30). Moreover, "ever since the beginning of the seventies all industrialized countries have had difficulties in reaching satisfactory growth rates. And the prospects for the eighties look even worse" (p. 195).[1]

1

So too, the postwar harmony among the industrialized capitalist countries, which, in reality, represented acquiescence to the dominance of the American economy, has dissolved. An increasingly strident competitive tone and an economic policy of national advantage have appeared. Long dormant antagonisms are resurfacing.

It is in this atmosphere, and largely as a response to systemic crisis in the world business system, that the new information technologies are being introduced into most of the developed market economies.

It is not surprising that relationships between these two phenomena are eagerly sought. One possible connection finds expression in this question: Can the new information technologies provide a restoration of general systemic growth and stability approximating the situation in the two decades after World War II? Or are the developments in information generation, processing, transmission, storage, and retrieval more likely to intensify strains in the system and create new problems that make stabilization unrealizable for the advanced market economies?

Western political leaders and policy-makers are unanimous in believing in the efficacy of the new technologies to lessen, if not overcome, current industrial stagnation and depression. The optimism is equally strong on both sides of the Atlantic.

EUROPE

In France, currently experiencing its deepest postwar crisis, the President of the Republic has made scientific research, and attention to information technology in particular, national priorities, and invested them with an urgent sense of mission. Addressing a national colloquium on Research and Technology in January 1982, Francois Mitterrand declared:

> In order to get out of the crisis, research constitutes one of the essential keys. It is the key to renovation. Such a gigantic effort of research will permit France to take her place among the few nations capable of controlling their technology and, in particular, protecting their independence...Electronics... in conjunction with the work of French scholarship will place our country in the first rank.[2]

In implementation of the presidential statement, France is devoting an increasingly large slice of its gross national product to research and development. Simultaneously, the government has announced a national program to cable the country. One million four hundred thousand households are scheduled to be linked to cable by 1985.[3]

The cable effort is dedicated explicitly to job creation, along with the hope of gaining export markets for French equipment, expertise, and programming. The programming required for the huge increase in channels made available by cable is expected to be supported by both advertising and viewer charges.[4]

In the United Kingdom, the hope that the new information technologies will supply the stimulus for stopping and reversing the slide of that economy is no less pronounced. The Hunt Committee Report on Cable Television, published in October 1982, endorsed the rapid cabling of English households.[5] It also gave a full government encouragement to British electronics equipment producers and video and film program-makers.

Britain's Home Secretary, Leon Brittan, summed up the Thatcher government's expectations for cable TV: "Cabling Britain will be an investment in tomorrow's growth and jobs, and the country's future. . . ."[6]

A writer in the *Times* (London) amplified this:

> The Government believes that such services could provide the infrastructure for a new industry in Britain with the potential to create thousands of new jobs and fresh export opportunities. Large markets could be created not only for the cable equipment suppliers and the consumer electronics industry, but also for the makers of films and television programmes, the suppliers of information services, and the marketing and advertising industries.[7]

In anticipation of this fact, conferences are being arranged to interest investors in the expected electronics boom. Glossy brochures announce that "Opportunities are boundless for a new breed of electronics entrepreneur."[8]

The general public, too, is fed large doses of extravagant claims for the new electronic instrumentation. 1982 was declared "Information Technology Year" in the United Kingdom. A poll conducted to assess the 12-month publicity campaign the Government organized, announced with satisfaction toward the end of the year that ". . .two-thirds of the people in Britain are *now* convinced that information technology will cause wide-ranging changes in society and two-thirds of those think the changes will be for the better."[9]

Not content with organizing national campaigns to rouse public enthusiasm, the government is supporting a range of academic research projects "on ways of encouraging acceptance" of the new technologies. The Department of Trade and Industry has invited the Social Science Research Council to handle the program with the objective being "the formulation of generalizable lessons for industry and government on how to secure greater acceptance of new technologies by developing their positive aspects and minimizing their negative aspects. . ."[10]

In West Germany, there are similar high expectations. The director of the country's first 35-channel commercial TV cable system in Ludwigshafen, assures, "Cable will create jobs. The economic aspect is incentive."

Nationally, the new head of Germany's Bundespost, the public government agency of Posts, Telephones and Telegraphs (PTT), repeats the refrain: "Employment is a first priority. . .Providing employment is a real good of this [cable and telecommunications] area."[11]

To complete the Western European picture, Gaston Thorn, the president of the European Community Commission, submitted a report in the fall of 1982, recommending revitalization of the 10-nation European Community by way of stimulating the high technology industries, particularly the aeronautical, electronics, and telecommunications fields.[12]

NORTH AMERICA

Across the Atlantic, the tone is equally buoyant. In Canada, troubled by the highest unemployment in forty years, the Minister of Communications, Francis Fox, informed an audience of business communicators in Montreal:

> At a time when microelectronics is emerging as the world's major industry, both in size and growth rate, Canada must not only retain a growing share of its own marketplace, but must also gain an appropriate share of the global market...Canada cannot afford to miss this opportunity...we must apply the new technologies to modernize our existing business and manufacturing operations and to create new jobs in emerging industries.[13]

Belief that the new high technology industries, especially electronics, can supply the vigor that is missing in an economy developed somewhat earlier in the United States. The decaying, older industrial base prompted early receptivity to the promotion of what were called the "sunrise" industries, as contrasted with those for whom the sun had almost set. Already in the last years of the Carter administration, the talk was of "revitalization." Venturous folk suggested that the new information industries could become the basis of a new international division of labor. In this design, U.S. leadership would be installed at the apex of the new order.[14]

The succeeding administration, despite a different rhetoric, has provided an enormous impetus to creating a still more advanced and powerful information-communication technology. In the 1.6 trillion dollar five-year military budget that the Reagan government hopes will awe the Soviets, communications research and development activities enjoy a large share of the expenditures.[15]

Democrats, too, have pounced on high technology as the answer to the domestic economic crisis. An economic policy paper issued by congressional Democrats in fall of 1982, called for the government "...to play a leadership role in easing our transition from a manufacturing-based economy to one that is increasingly involved in technology, information and services."

These "Atari Democrats"—named after the computer game company before it fell on hard times—urged increased national expenditures on research and development and seek assistance for the stimulation of the high technology-electronics sectors.[16]

However, the new technology consensus transcends party politics. Admiral Bobby R. Inman, the former deputy director of the CIA, and, later, head of the super-secret National Security Agency (NSA), current president of the Microelectronics and Computer-Technology Corporation (MCC), a new, "nonprofit cooperative" venture of some sixteen U.S. micro-electronics companies, held up this incentive for embarking on the race to bigger and more powerful computers:

> The information-handling industry is growing at a rate of 15 percent a year. That's a trillion-dollar industry in the 1990s. That's 15 million jobs.

But this pot of gold at the end of the micro-electronics rainbow is attainable, Mr. Inman cautions, "only if we lead."[17]

No less concerned, the United States National Academy of Sciences, in 1983, issued a cautionary report, urging rapid governmental action to prevent further erosion of the American world technological lead, especially in the "frontier industries" such as micro-electronics, computers, new materials, robotics, and new biological techniques.[18]

In any event, the race by way of electronics to escape crisis is well under way in the Western industralized world. It receives added stimulus from the remarkably successful Japanese electronics initiatives. In early 1984, the *New York Times,* (February 17, 1984), ran a front-page story with this scare headline: "Big Japanese Gain in Computers Seen: Scientists Fear New Devices Will End U.S. Dominance." Cables are being laid. Fibre optics production is being pushed. Satellites are being catapulted into space. And computer games are familiarizing the younger generation with electronic gadgetry.

SUPPOSED BENEFITS

Economic stagnation and the pressure of competition in the world market are the driving forces behind most of these developments.[19] The publicists, however—political, academic, and commercial—find it necessary to explain recent action in electronics in more reassuring terms to the general public. The Canadian Communications Minister puts it this way:

> Governments everywhere face the social reality of a strong undercurrent of distrust of technology among working men and women who are concerned about their ability to make a living in a high technology world.
>
> As professional communicators, you will recognize the magnitude of the communications task that faces all of us in educating Canadians to overcome these fears. In this time of unprecedented economic difficulty, how do we explain to people working in factories that the introduction of robots on the factory floor will benefit their families in the long run?[20]

Thus, the new information age, we are told, will not only prevent job loss but actually will create innumerable new work opportunities. Internationally, the increased interdependence between nations resulting from the new communications networks will reduce frictions and quarrels. Domestically, reinvigorated political participation may be expected through electronic plebiscitary processes. To complete the good tidings, according to this formula for positive thinking, there will be enhanced individual choice and wider access all around to information stockpiles.

Actually, what is occurring at the institutional and structural levels of national and international economy, make these expectations not merely unrealistic but delusionary.

IMPACT OF THE NEW TECHNOLOGIES

What the impact of the burgeoning electronic activities will be on any individual economy requires a detailed, precise analysis of the specific circumstances—historical, political, economic, and cultural—applying to that society. Failing this, the best that can be done here is to offer a few general considerations that may provide an initial framework in which to develop a detailed, specific country analysis.

ROLE OF PRIVATE SECTOR

The international scramble into high technology electronics is characterized by the dominant role of what has come to be known as the transnational corporation (TNC). Though governments are active in providing initial and back-up support, it is the TNC that is the decisive mover in the new information technology sector. The state acts as guarantor and insurer, taking all the risks and financing the outlays from the general public's taxes. The TNC takes over when the uncertainty disappears and the profit picture brightens. There is variation in this pattern, to be sure, but overall it is a fair description of what has been happening in recent decades.

Accordingly, once the technology has been tested and is in place, capitalist decision-making at the level of the transnational or national enterprise, becomes the guiding feature of the new information sector. Production is geared to profitability, and market criteria override any other concerns. The world market cannot and does not concern itself with French unemployment, Canadian workers displaced by robots, or English plant closings.

It is revealing that each of the countries' hopes and plans for gaining advantage from the new electronics technologies is not dependent on domestic, planned utilization of the new instrumentation and processes. They have all thrown their lot in with the international market, intending to gain advantage and large chunks of what is hoped will be a growing sector. But in doing so, each participant loses control of its project and is thrown up against others, with no holds barred. Market saturation is inevitable. The TNCs will shift their production to the most economical sites. National expectations of significant gains will, in most instances, be disappointed.

The French case is especially instructive. Though the domestic rhetoric about the information age emphasizes independent decision-making and national autonomy, and the information sector is largely state-owned, the general economic policies adopted by the Socialist government are unambiguously tied to the international market and follow traditional market practices. Planning in one sector of the economy therefore, however advanced that segment is, is bound to be an exercise in futility.

When the Minister of Finance, for example, announced a financial program in early 1983 to cope with the current economic crisis, he stressed that: "We are maintaining an open economy."[21] This means, in brief, that the French economy will be exposed to the calculus of transnational capital. It will be the latter that will decide to invest or disinvest, to allow French products into the world market or exclude them. Who, for instance, will buy French information goods and services if they are available elsewhere more cheaply? And if this happens, how can investment and employment in French information industries be maintained, especially if foreign markets are also preempted?

A striking example of how the system operates globally was provided at the end of 1982, when the affiliate of Warner Communications, the Atari Company, experienced a fall-off from what had been fabulous sales. The management response was almost instantaneous. Plants in Santa Clara, California, employing 1700 workers, were shut down and the workers released. The company announced it was moving its manufacturing to plants in Hong Kong and Taiwan—where it already has facilities. "It was a difficult decision but it had to be done to cut costs," one Atari spokesman said. "Wages," he added, "are an important factor in the equation, and so are taxes, real estate and other costs."[22]

LOSS OF SOVEREIGNTY

There are still other consequences of allowing the TNCs to be the primary actors. Whatever new constellations and coalitions of economic power emerge in the new information technology sector, the transfer of authority from the national state to the transnational entity continues, and, indeed, may be accelerating.[23]

This is so partly because the transnationals are the chief beneficiaries and employers of the new information processes and instrumentation. This fact permits them to command still greater capabilities for avoiding and sometimes countermanding national policies that they may find onerous.

Claude Cheysson, the French foreign minister, speaking to the 12th Congress of the Socialist Parties of the European Community, made this point emphatically:

> The transnational companies have the monopoly of analysis and strategic definitions at the world level—Neither governments nor trade unions, nor political forces have this capability.... This is an intolerable situation.... Their strategy escapes us.[24]

It is predictable that conflicts concerning national sovereignty will become more abrasive. This will be so not only in the cultural and political spheres that have generally received most of the attention, but now in the national economy itself. For example, the arrest, quickly countermanded, of Argentina's leading banker, was prompted by the charge that he had compromised the nation's sovereignty when he accepted the terms of the International Monetary Fund (IMF) which permitted monitoring and intervention in Argentinian affairs by external creditor agencies.[25]

With powerful intra-company global communications networks at its disposal, the transnational enterprise today is in a position to make production, investment, funds transfer, and related decisions on a global scale. There is no reason why the TNCs' global considerations should be in accord with the plans or perceived needs of any one of the many nation states in which the TNC is active. In the clash between transnational and national interest there is no guarantee that the latter will be sustained.

Additionally, the commercialization of information that the private control of the new information technologies encourages—information as a commodity—further enhances the power of the transnational firms and correspondingly diminishes the authority of the national state. Access to information, more than ever, becomes a factor of wealth and income. The general public and sometimes the state itself are progressively excluded.

Though this development is still in a relatively early phase, its presence and movement are markedly demonstrable. The division inside the society between information "haves" and "have nots" deepens just as it does between nations, making the less-developed ones—which in the information age means the overwhelming majority—still more dependent on the few information generators, processors, and transmitters.

In a word, the new information technologies, as they are being installed and administered, are creating highly unstable structures and relationships, nationally and internationally. Deepening inequality and dispossession hardly constitute a formula for long-lasting equilibrium.

BASIS OF CONFLICT

Not surprisingly, the old state systems of communications administration in Western Europe, the PTTs, are being pressed by the TNC-led forces of privatization and commercialization. A Citicorp executive indicates some of the rules the TNCs are seeking to legitimate. At least three of the concepts deemed essential by the transnational corporation, he says, collide directly with the sovereignty of nations:

- Ownership: Users of the networks must be able to own at least their point of entry vehicle to the network, and preferably a portion of the backbone. In addition, the user should play a central role in administration.
- Flow: Communications must be able to cross international boundaries without respect for its contents. Any attempt to levy taxes or tariffs on the flow of information must be based upon volume and not content.
- Responsibility: Management of the global networks should reside with the owners and operators, as opposed to government agencies. The challenge to the unlimited sovereign power of nation-states brought about by the technological realities of global communications may be perceived as a matter requiring tight surveillance and possibly direct intervention by governments. Here we must remind ourselves that money is a form of information. Thus, restrictions on world communications become restrictions on the property rights of individuals and corporations alike. As a result of highspeed communications, a new relationship has emerged between the right of free speech and property rights.[26]

Describing what he calls "The Progress of Privatization in World Telecommunications," one writer concludes: "The United States, the center of the transnational business system, is for that very reason also the historical source and current center of the privatization trend."[27]

CONSEQUENCES OF PRIVATIZATION

However, privatization of communications facilities and processes brings with it certain inevitabilities. The most important of these is the imposition of market criteria. These, in turn, supply the answers to such questions as how to pay for the creation and use of satellite transmission systems with greatly increased channel capacity, for the introduction and use of cable, and for the creation and use of electronically operated data banks.

In the case of television transmission, either with satellite or cable or both, the ultimate sources of revenues in a private system are the sponsor and the viewer. The sponsor is almost always the transnational enterprise through the intermediary of the advertising agency, generally another TNC. When the viewer pays, it is through special charges for what may be either general reception of a channel or for a specific program.

According to this dynamic, when national policy encourages the creation of communications networks under private control, as is happening across

Western Europe and in other parts of the world, the new circuits are being turned over mostly to transnational enterprises for their messages, and the people in the countries concerned are being delivered up as targets to international advertisers and image transmitters.

There are other benefits as well to be gained by U.S. transnationals from the communications build-ups in Europe and elsewhere. American equipment companies are forming joint ventures to penetrate the European markets.[28] U.S. software producers and entertainment and computer programming firms are no less active and anticipate heavy sales in the new outlets. Their expectations are grounded in the new programming capacities being established:

> Countries that, like England, seem eager to press ahead with cable and DBS, will soon find themselves with far more air-time than available programming. The United States remains the world's leading producer of television entertainment. The U.S. networks are not only geared up to provide programming to new systems abroad, but regard export as a major factor in their future growth and financial health.[29]

CONCLUSIONS

Whether these policies will overcome stagnation and depression in the short run is an open question. Certainly, some national expectations are going to be disappointed. Looking beyond the next few years, it is safe, I believe, to conclude that the present economic crisis will assume far greater breadth, combining economic, national, and cultural dimensions.

The massive anticipated increases in global advertising by the TNCs are almost a guarantor of this. The expansion of communication networks and facilities, now being undertaken "to escape the crisis," figure strongly in the projected surge of worldwide advertising from 110 billion dollars in 1980 to 780 billion dollars in 2000 A.D. According to *Advertising Age,* "The advertising strategies now being employed successfully in the US will inevitably spread around the world as media availabilities and consumer purchasing power grow."[30]

These expenditures are intended to unleash consumerism of the kind that now inundates American life. But global circumstances are different. Encouraging consumerism, and the inappropriate production of goods and services that attend it, promises to produce cataclysmic encounters in a world possessing vast, unmet elemental needs.

There are other, no less powerful disequilibrating forces at work. What are the prospects, for instance, of huge sales of electronic hardware that the advanced market economies are hoping to make to the less industrialized world? Given the limitation of the home markets of most of the already industrialized economies, the availability of foreign sales constitutes a central assumption in the plans of those expecting to relieve the crisis in the industrialized metropoles. "Most advanced countries," one account notes, "virtually shut out foreign suppliers of public telecommunications equipment."[31]

This takes on special significance when it is recognized that the developed market economies give no indication at this time that they are intending to make use of the new instrumentation for planned, carefully staged internal development. In fact, it is taken for granted by the big information hardware companies that they can only survive in a world market. The Director-General of the French computer and informatics company, C.I.I. Honeywell-Bull, in a year-end company report for 1982, wrote: "The informatics industry can only be conceived of on a world scale."[32]

Can the developing nations provide the mass market so desperately required by the crisis-enveloped Western economies? Present economic conditions make this doubtful, now, and into the foreseeable future. Overwhelmed by debt, obliged to pay interest charges that consume a huge fraction of their export revenues, as well as practically all new borrowed funds, most developing countries are now able to pay for only absolutely vital imports.

Still, just as Europeans and North Americans are told that the problems of industrial depression can be overcome with the new information technologies, a similar message is fashioned for the people of the Third World, yet one which takes into account the inescapable differences in the latter's situation. In the Third World version of the promise of information technology, it is claimed that the new instrumentation will enable huge jumps to be made in the developmental process.

The adherents of this view urge that funds be made available through the international banking system so that new instrumentation can be purchased.

Actively promoting this policy in the poor world is the Rome-based Intergovernmental Bureau of Informatics (IBI), an international grouping of a few dozen, mostly Third World nations, with some West European participation and growing American interest.

IBI Director, Fermin Bernasconi, argues that the Third World can avoid longterm subservience to the advanced industrialized countries only if it builds up rapidly its own informational infrastructure. At the same time, Bernasconi points out the benefits that will accrue to the developed nations from such a build-up.

These are implicit in the Bernasconi recommendation that Third World countries should allocate a larger fraction of their resources to the acquisition of the new information technology. He hopes to see the informatics market in the developing countries increase from 2 to 3 billion dollars annually to 10 to 12 billion dollars a year.[33] This prospect, however uncertain, cannot fail to whet the appetites of equipment and software producers in Europe and North America. To start the process moving, the IBI seeks initial funds from the industrialized centers.

Whether the IBI's ambitious program can be realized is still unclear. Yet if it, or some similar development, in fact does materialize, new kinds of problems will soon enough be manifest.

For one thing, what will be the impact of automated equipment on countries with already vast numbers of unemployed labor crowded miserably around cities swollen with homeless migrants? Merely a drop in the price of oil forces oil-exporting Nigeria to push hundreds of thousands of immigrants out of its territory. What may be expected of automated production lines in South East Asia and Latin America?

In this perspective, the plans and programs now underway to expand communications structures and industries in order to overcome industrial slackness and unemployment, are laying the foundations for global upheavals of immeasurable intensity.

There is no intentionality in all this and certainly no deliberate misanthropy. The actors are going about their business in the best way they know. Yet strengthening private transnational enterprise, and the consumerism this system induces, are the explosive ingredients for future conflagrations.

A recent study concluded with this question: "Can the Information Revolution reverse the trends of unequal development begun during the 16th century with the advent of capitalism and solidified by the Industrial Revolution? This will depend on how well the emerging strategies for the information regime developed by nations can balance technologies."[34]

A conclusive answer may still be premature, but on the basis of evidence now accumulating, briefly referred to at the beginning of this chapter, the Information Revolution is proceeding much like the Industrial Revolution that preceded it. The burdens are unequally shared. The benefits are unequally divided. How long this will continue and under what circumstances it may change are matters that will be returned to.

One conclusion does seem warranted. The likelihood of achieving a stable world system—the prerequisite for the successful operation of an information-based global order under transnational corporate direction—recedes measurably with each initiative in the construction of that order.

NOTES TO CHAPTER ONE

1. G. Friedrichs and A. Schaff, *Micro-Electronics and Society,* New York, Mentor, 1983, pp. 30 and 195.

2. Francois Mitterrand, Official Opening of Colloque National en Recherche et Technologie, January 13, 1982, La Documentation Francaise, 1982. (Translation by the author)

3. Official Communique of the Council of Ministers, *Le Monde,* November 5, 1982.

4. Jean-Francois Lacan, "L'Enjeu culturel des nouveaux medias," *Le Monde,* Part 1, October 15, 1982, p. 31. Part 2, October 16, 1982, p. 27.

5. Report of the Inquiry Into Cable Expansion and Broadcasting Policy, October 1982, London, HMSO, Command 8679 (Hunt Committee Report).

6. "Full Speed Ahead for Cable TV—Brittan," The *Guardian,* July 1, 1983.

7. Bill Johnstone, "Dramatic Effect of New Facilities," *Times* (London), October 6, 1982.

8. "Investing In European Communication Cable Technology," Two-day International Conference, arranged by Investment and Property Studies Limited, The Hilton International Hotel, London, November 1-2, 1982.

9. Peter Large, "Two-Thirds of Britain Thinks the IT is a Hit," The *Guardian,* December 8, 1982 (Emphasis added).

10. *Times Higher Education Supplement* (THES), August 28, 1983.

11. Michael Schrage, "Europe Turning to Cable TV for Fiscal Boost," *International Herald Tribune,* November 16, 1982.

12. Axel Krause, "EC Proposes Reforms to Revitalize Industry," *International Herald Tribune,* December 4-5, 1982.

13. Francis Fox, "The Role of New Technologies in Economic Recovery," Address to the International Association of Business Communicators, Montreal, Quebec, September 20, 1982.

14. Herbert I. Schiller, *Who Knows: Information in The Age of the Fortune 500,* Norwood, New Jersey, Ablex Publishing Corporation, 1981, chapter 1.

15. The *New York Times,* three articles, October 17, 18, 19, 1982. Richard Halloran, "U.S. Plans Big Spending Increase for Military Operations in Space" (October 17th); Philip M. Boffey, "Pressures Are Increasing for Arms Race In Space" (October 18th); John Noble Wilford, "Military's Future In Space: A Matter of War or Peace" (October 19th).

16. Jake Kirchner, "Democrats Set High-Tech Goals," *Computerworld,* October 4, 1982.

17. "Computer Consortium," The *New York Times,* May 16, 1983.

18. Philip M. Boffey, "U.S. Priority on Technology Is Urged," The *New York Times,* April 15, 1983.

19. "The crisis and the international competition require the companies in the industrialized countries to improve their competitiveness. Electronics and its many applications allow gains in productivity; robotics and office automation affect the secondary and tertiary levels," writes a *Le Monde* correspondent, Jean-Michel Quatrepoint, "Technologie: un effort gigantesque de formation," *Le Monde,* January 4, 1983, p. 11.

20. Francis Fox, *op cit.*

21. Paul Lewis, "Austerity Plans Adopted in France Include Tax Rises," The *New York Times,* March 26, 1983.

22. "Atari to Eliminate 1,700 Jobs in California. Will Move Manufacturing to the Far East," The *Wall Street Journal,* European Edition, February 24, 1983.

23. Each day brings news of ambitious plans for global reshuffling of power. AT&T makes overtures to Philips and Olivetti. Thomson seeks a merger with Grundig. IBM organizes consortia in the U.K. and Australia, and so on.

24. "M. Cheysson denonce la puissance des firmes multinationales," *Le Monde,* November 14–15, 1982.

25. The *New York Times,* October 5, 1983.

26. Kenneth L. Phillips,Citicorp, N.A., "Comments" at the Institute in International Telecommunications Policy, 1980.

27. Dan Schiller, "The Progress of Privatization in World Telecommunications," Paper presented to the International Association for Mass Communication Research, 13th General Assembly and Scientific Conference, September 6–10, 1982, Paris, Communication Technology Section.

28. John Tagliabue, "Wiring Europe for Cable TV: U.S. Concerns Join the Rush," The *New York Times,* June 25, 1983.

29. Henry Geller, "The Old World Enters The New Age," *Channels,* March/April, 1983, p. 46.

30. Robert J. Coen, "Vast U.S. and Worldwide Ad Expenditures Expected," *Advertising Age,* November 13, 1980, pp. 1–16.

31. Bob Hagerty, "A.T. and T. Faces Obstacles To Foreign Push," The *International Herald Tribune,* January 6, 1983.

32. J. M. Quatrepoint, "Informatique: le quitte ou double de C.I.I. Honeywell-Bull," *Le Monde,* February 26, 1983, p. 26. (Translation of the author.)

33. Jake Kirchner, "IBI Chief: Third World, Europe Share Interests," *Computerworld,* June 6, 1983, pp. 15–16.

34. Belinda Canton and Herbert S. Dordick, "Information Strategies and International Trade Policy," *TDR,* Vol. 6, No. 6, September, 1982, p. 312.

Chapter Two

Communication Against an Insurgent World*

Crisis management is the priority task of the 1980s and new information technology supplies the instrumentation to accomplish it. Such is the prevailing view in a good part of Western Europe, North America, and Japan. It follows, therefore, that massive dosages of what the French call "informatisation," are being applied to the industrial crisis afflicting these regions.

Yet there is another kind of crisis beside the industrial one, no less urgent, confronting the world business system. The national liberation, anti-imperialist, and socialist movements of the 20th century, which have developed with special vigor since the end of World War II, constitute the other crisis.

The new technology is intended to handle this crisis as well. Actually, since mid-century, it has served as a vital means of combating these movements and facilitating the expansion of the world business system. Information and communication systems have been applied to global surveillance, rapid deployment of armed force, market penetration for transnational corporations, and a worldwide ideological barrage.

Given the centrality of information and communication processes to the military task of beating back a near global resistance to prevailing economic and cultural institutional arrangements, the need to examine the informational-military connection is long overdue. If there are indeed, "blind spots"[1] in communication research, one of the largest must be the sphere of the military involvement in the "Information Revolution." It is to this "blind-spot" that this chapter is directed.

In 1981, the Edward R. Murrow Symposium had as its subject: "The Information Society: Social and Ethical Issues." The major concern of the

---

* Adapted from "Information for What Kind of Society?" by Herbert I. Schiller. In *Telecommunication: Issues and Choices for Society* edited by Jerry L. Salvaggio. Copyright © 1983 by Longman Inc. Reprinted by permission of Longman Inc., New York.

symposium was expressed in an initial statement by the conference organizer: "A communications revolution such as is taking place at the present
time, will have a tremendous impact on our society and will create certain
social and ethical problems."[2]

The statement assumes that if we're not careful, new developments in
telecommunications may have unintended and potentially harmful impacts
and consequences in the future. It is useful, according to the symposium's
organizer, to consider these possibilities as early as possible.

In general, such anticipatory thinking is unusual and deserves credit. But
in this instance the focus on the future may create more problems than it
solves because it does not take account of current reality but shifts attention
away from it. The question to be considered is not what may happen if a
new communication technology runs amok. The issue is much more stark
and immediate. It is, How do we check a communication technology that is
already running amok and that has had this tendency to do so built into it
from the outset? In short, how do we deal with communication systems that
have been conceived, designed, built, and installed with the primary objectives being the maintenance of economic privilege and advantage and the
prevention of the kind of social change that would overturn and eliminate
this privilege?

Developments in telecommunications since the Second World War, with
few exceptions, have satisfied these negative objectives. Yet is is amazing
how little this has been perceived by those whose task it is to chart and ana-
lyze such phenomena. The prime example is the vast military outlay that has
been made by the U.S. government over the last forty years. Communication
technologies have received a great and growing share of these expenditures.

The attention and favor extended to communications—now institutionalized in an information industry—have not been due to chance. Still it
is puzzling that the armaments boom and its runoff on communication
technologies escape the attention and concern of researchers and workers
whose area of interest is at the center of these developments. It is hardly a
secret that the armaments output in America has reached staggering levels.[3]
Nobel laureate, Hannes Alfven, suggests that "perhaps it is appropriate to
give the *Bulletin* [of the Atomic Scientists' doomsday] clock a third hand
which would show the seconds we have left in the count down..."[4]

Despite this, each new administration, following the course of previous
administrations, has discovered a giant gap in American military prepared-
ness. The ante is being raised once again. In the five-year period from 1981
to 1985, more than 1½ trillion dollars (1,500 billion dollars) will be poured
into military expenditures—on top of past trillions. A good chunk of this
astronomical outlay will go to the production of new telecommunication
systems.[5]

Simon Ramo, founder and currently director of TRW, one of the corporate recipients of the population's tax money for military electronics

products, explains the impact of the planned military expenditures on the information and communication sector:

> Our military expenditures will probably increase as a percentage of the GNP over the next decade, and this could be extremely pertinent and beneficial to our leadership position in information technology, especially in computers and communications. This is because the right way for us to enhance our military strength in weapons systems is through superior communication, command, control and overall utilization of our weapons systems—functions that depend on superior information technology.[6]

Unlike most communication researchers, Simon Ramo has the priorities in their proper order.

Actually, what Ramo is anticipating has been the practice throughout most of the past four decades. The entire electronics industry is an outcome of military subsidy and encouragement.

The developments in electronics are inseparable from war and preparations for war. From the outset, the military officer who oversaw the construction of the first viable computer in the United States, the Electronic Numerical Integrator and Calculator (ENIAC), confirms that:

> It was the influence of the war that matured the field of electronics. The tremendous advances in radar and fire control work changed electronics from a hobby into a great industry.[7]

Actually, the production of ENIAC, begun in 1943 at the University of Pennsylvania, is indicative of the course of development of information technology over the last forty years.

The Army sponsored and financed ENIAC and assigned an Ordinance Officer, Dr. Herman Goldstine, to the original engineering team of Mauchly and Eckert that constructed the machine. When ENIAC was completed in 1946, it was installed at the Aberdeen Proving Ground in Maryland to serve the requirements of its sponsor, the Ballistics Research Laboratory.

The first commercial computer, UNIVAC, was also a Mauchly-Eckert creation and again the government supplied the market. Four of the first six machines made were delivered to the United States Census Bureau in 1951.

The career paths of the individuals involved in the construction of the first computers in America constitute a model of the institutional connections that characterize the electronics field. They demonstrate the interlocks of the military establishment, the corporate world, and the laboratories of academia. Goldstine, for example, after his assignment to ENIAC was completed, went to the Institute of Advanced Study in Princeton where he collaborated with John Von Neumann. From their work came a design that set the standard for a series of computers, AVIDAC, ORDVAC, ORACLE, SILLIAC, ILLIAC, MANIAC, JOHNNIA, and the IBM 701.

Little has changed in the basic pattern of government support through military expenditures and close corporate and academic collaboration in the production of designs and equipment of electronic hardware since the early post-World War II period. The technology has become more powerful and the systems more sophisticated. But the underlying relationships and connections are as strong as ever.

In the race to develop a "supercomputer" in the 1980s, for example, the Defense Advanced Research Projects Agency (DARPA), the unit which manages the Defense Department's basic and applied research programs, is taking the lead. At the same time, the Department of Energy (DOE) which supervises nuclear power and weapons research, is one of the main purchasers of the enormously expensive equipment. The National Aeronautical and Space Administration (NASA) also is interested in large machines as instrumentation assisting its ongoing work on advanced aircraft design.[8]

While the direct military link to computer development and sales remains in place, the connections to academia and the corporate sector have become, if possible, closer than ever.

In July 1983, *Newsweek* reported that:

> The Pentagon's Defense Advanced Research Projects Agency (DARPA) is, more than any other single agency in the world, responsible for the shape of advanced computer science today—and for many technologies now in widespread commercial use. Over the past 20 years, DARPA has poured half a billion dollars into computer research, in the process virtually creating the science of artificial intelligence.[9]

Six months later, DARPA announced a new program to spend an additional 600 million dollars to develop artificial intelligence systems and computer technology. The report in *Science* noted that the DARPA plan "comes none too soon for many members of industry and academia, who have been pressing for more money in artificial intelligence research."[10]

To be sure, the military influence on academia extends far beyond electronics research but it is especially active and substantial in this area. As for the military–industrial complex, it is a longstanding phenomenon in the U.S. economy, reaching back at least to the Second World War.[11] Yet here too, electronics constitute a current site of powerful linkages.

One striking example, mentioned previously, is the Microelectronics and Computer-Technology Corporation, headed by Admiral Bobby R. Inman, to carry on advanced research in electronics, some of which is pointed to the development of a supercomputer.

Laser research is another field of activity which brings together the military and the corporate worlds. The chief contractors for the Pentagon in this area are TRW, Mr. Ramo's company, Rockwell International, Hughes Aircraft, and Lockheed.[12]

The farreaching involvement of the military in communications can be gauged from a *partial* listing of the programs cited in the Secretary of Defense's Annual Report to Congress[13] for the fiscal year, 1984:

Satellite Communications Systems
Ground Wave Emergency Network
Strategic Bomber Communications
Extremely low-frequency communications (for submarines)
Non-strategic nuclear force communication
Combat Identification Systems
E-3A Airborne Warning and Control Systems (AWACS)
Relocatable Over-the-Horizon Radar
TR-1 Reconnaissance Aircraft
Joint Surveillance and Target Attack Radar Systems
Single Channel Ground and Airborne Radio Systems
Tactical HF Communications
Defense Electronic Countermeasures
Mutual Support Electronic Countermeasures
Threat Warning
Destructive countermeasures
Communications Jamming
Navigation and location
Defense Satellite communications systems
Defense switched network
Worldwide Digital System Architecture
Secure Voice Improvement Program
Consolidated Crypto-logic Program
Special Reconnaissance Activities
Defense Foreign Intelligence

If nothing else, this enumeration is suggestive of the range of research and development projects in communication and information that have kept battalions of American scientists and engineers employed for decades and have produced a flood of information technologies and processes.

The first communication satellite system was a military effort. Most of the satellites in the sky today are providing military data. In January 1981, *Science* reported that "the Army soon expects to have 13,000 computers, the Navy, 33,000 and the Air Force, 40,000. The software bill for military computers last year came to more than $3 billion."[14]

So great is the Department of Defense's utilization of this huge arsenal of computers that it is compelled to finance the development of a standardized computer language—ADA—to overcome its present reliance on more than 1000 computer languages. As things now stand, "Navy computers cannot easily communicate with Air Force computers."[15] But in this area as well, military influence has had a long history. "The Pentagon," *Science* reminds us, "was the driving force behind the development of COBOL (Common Business-Oriented Language), which was introduced in 1959 and is today used extensively around the world."[16]

Still, the development of computer languages is but one debt the information age owes to its military parentage. Much more direct, though far less accessible than ADA or COBOL, is the dense U.S. electronic espionage network that encircles the world, not excluding national territory. This, too, is a creation made possible by the most sophisticated communication technologies.

The supersecret National Security Agency (NSA), for example, works largely with satellites, microwave stations, and computers.

> Its mission includes cracking enemy codes, developing unbreakable ciphers for the United States and, most importantly, monitoring, translating, and analyzing worldwide communications among nations, selected foreign citizens and some corporations.[17]

In 1976, NSA controlled 2000 overseas listening posts.[18] Much more than a listening post, Australia is practically an American preserve. The country serves as a continental base across the Pacific Ocean, for a full complement of NSA electronic installations, to be directed against the Soviet Union and any other perceived adversary. It is described by one Australian reporter as a "massive eavesdropping on Australian communications. . .conducted by facilities dotted around Australia as a part of a U.S. nuclear war fighting machine that has been nurtured on Australian soil by [an] inner circle."[19] Desmond Ball, who documented the U.S. electronic presence in Australia, inscribed his book "For a Sovereign Australia."[20]

Australians are not alone in having their communication—personal, commercial, and governmental—intercepted and monitored. The NSA performs the same functions with abandon around the world including inside the United States. An NSA intercept station outside London, for example, checks all incoming and outgoing U.K.-European communication traffic. The annual budget for the operation of this global assemblage of modern communication technology is a secret. One estimate, by the House Government Operations Committee in 1976, reported an annual expenditure of 15 billion dollars.[21]

What does this huge sum buy? Nothing less than what many generously call the "information society."

According to a report by Charles Morgan, who used data supplied elsewhere by Harrison Salisbury, ". . .in 1973 alone, NSA retrieved a total of 23,346,587, individual communications. . ." Morgan notes with astonishment that this figure is "not the number of individual communications *intercepted;* it is the number of communications *retrieved* for full study by the NSA."[22]

By 1980, the existence of the National Reconnaissance Office had been revealed. Still another supersecret military agency, its mission "is to oversee the development and operation of spy satellites used to photograph foreign territory and to monitor international communications."[23] Its budget exceeds 2 billion dollars a year. Its satellites in the 1960s and 1970s were used "to photograph antiwar demonstrations and urban riots..."[24]

The CIA deserves mention at this point. It is no wallflower in the business of electronic surveillance. Though it is no longer fashionable to bring up Watergate, it will be remembered that the crew of bunglers recruited by the Nixon high command came out of the agency.

In sum, a great amount of the activity, a good share of the content, and the general thrust of what is now defined as the information age, represent military and intelligence connections.

Scholarly work in communications puts these matters differently. In what has become a familiar argument, the duality and ambiguity of the new communication instrumentation is emphasized. The potential for constructive as well as destructive ends is insisted upon. For instance, Anthony Oettinger, director of Harvard's Program on Information Resources Policy, writes:

> Tensions will continue because of the close kinship among the technical means used for sometimes antithetical purposes—keeping peace or waging war, gathering intelligence or mapping agricultural and mineral resources, providing communications for trade or for military command and control.[25]

But is it appropriate or even relevant to ask if the new instrumentation is truly indifferent to the uses to which it is applied and whether it can be utilized for social and peaceful goals as well as its current applications to war and war preparations?

Given the prevailing structure of global industrial and military power, the communication revolution inevitably is the outcome of, and serves to sustain, the extensive efforts to maintain a worldwide system of economic advantage.

New information technologies have been invented, developed, and introduced to support the business component of this system and to enable a globe-girdling military communication network to be prepared to be the ultimate enforcer. In 1983, for example, Vice Admiral Gordon R. Hagler, the Navy's director of Command and Control, explained that "the commander of a naval battle group that includes an aircraft carrier, several surface ships and two or more submarines, *sends or receives 40,000 messages a month*. The Navy generally deploys eight battle groups."[26]

It it to facilitate these needs that accounts for the longstanding great support extended to communications research and development. As former Deputy Assistant Secretary for Human Rights and Social Affairs, Sarah Goddard Power explained these dynamics:

> Either we will design, produce, market and distribute the most advanced products and services spun off by the communications revolution—and, in so doing, reinforce our economic as well as political, social, and cultural *advan-*

tage—or we will increasingly find ourselves in the position of consumer and debtor to those who do...The question of how the world adapts to the communications revolution has been steadily moving up the list of international concerns over the last decade, and has now emerged as a major point of contention in East-West and North-South relationships.[27]

Maintaining and "reinforcing our advantage" are the explicit grounds that activate and accelerate the communications revolution. There is no ambiguity or dualism here. It is not a question of "either-or"...good technology use or bad technology use. It is solely a matter of developing and using the new communication technology for holding on to the economic benefits derived from a world system of power. For this reason, insistence on the potential and positive features of the current communication instrumentation is disingenuous at best.

To be sure, a part of the technology is used to produce consumer products, games, and "entertainment." Many of these are actually applications seeking a use. Assorted privateers of enterprise naturally make the most of the opportunities created by this technology.

It is also undeniable that the commercial utilization of telecommunications will affect employment in the private and public sectors. The character of work itself will change. Living patterns will alter. House, home, and family arrangements will change. What will not be different—not if the corporate-military directorate has anything to say about it—are basic relationships of authority, ownership, and hierarchy of skills.

All the same, domestically and internationally, the evolving communications industry is being hailed and promoted as efficient, problem solving, and liberating. The capability for enormously expanded generation and transmission of volumes of information, the technical feasibility of two-way communications, and the choice and diversity that new information technologies allegedly will provide, are publicized widely as realizable goals, affording hope to disadvantaged and excluded nations, classes, and people. These are not only unrealizable objectives. Under prevailing circumstances, their enunciation is misleading and deceptive. Other than for a few meritorious functions (libraries, medicine),[28] significant socially beneficial utilization of the new technologies requires societal restructuring. The notion that humanistic social change can be introduced incrementally, via the new technology, is unrealistic to the point of fantasy.

The social potential that may exist, and I stress the "may," in some of the new instrumentation can be developed appreciably only in totally different social-cultural-economic contexts. Claims, therefore, that the two-sidedness of the instrumentation—its potential for good or evil—necessitate its immediate development in the hope that the socially desirable side may be encouraged are either uninformed by history or, more likely, too well informed by special interest.

What forces other nations to board the electronics bandwagon is no simple desire for human improvement. It originates with the competitive drives of the world business system. It comes from the fear of being excluded from markets, losing employment, and being forced further down the economic ladder to deeper dependence. The deluge of new information equipment, processes, and products created by the staggering military outlays in the U.S. whips the world community into the game of follow-the-leader, regardless of need or utility.

Though hardly criticizing the process, it is neatly described by a British scientist, who the *Guardian* calls "an archetypal member of the technological establishment." Sir Ieuan Maddock explains why the United Kingdom cannot allow its electronics effort to proceed in an unhurried way:

> The problem is created by America and by its gigantic defense expenditure. The purchasing power of the Pentagon for high technology electronic products is comparable to the entire purchasing power of the UK. By concentrating public funds into this one industry, conscious of the need to maintain world leadership for strategic reasons, a freak industry has been produced, which spends an exceptional proportion of its turnover on research and development, is constantly out-dating its most recent products and is advancing the performance/cost ratio at a pace never experienced in any industry. Other countries have noted this and have set themselves the task of matching this by their own particular methods (Japan, France, W. Germany, Sweden). If the UK is to survive in this competition it will have to commit large resources and much national determination to the task.[29]

Accordingly, the world, especially the U.S.-administered part of the world, is being hooked into electronic circuitry that serves to keep things under control for the transnational corporate community of IBM–Chase Manhattan–Citicorp–Exxon–Arco–CBS–J. Walter Thompson and their friends. Transnational data flows within and among these business giants have become indispensable to the maintenance of the world business system. Additional networks thicken the connections and extend the system's influence.[30] The stronger the electronic networks established, the less likely the possibility for national autonomy and independent decision making, and the more likely an intensified patrolling and controlling of the Third World majority.[31]

Surveillance, intervention, and marketing are the near-certain outcomes of the utilization of new communication technologies, domestically and globally. The American public, half of which does not bother to vote in national elections, hears the good news that electronic referendums are around the corner. Sitting at home, in front of a domestic information utility, so-called, the happy citizen will be able to exercise innumerable inconsequential choices on an electronic console in the living room. This, we are told, constitutes the most advanced form of democracy.

Actually, business and marketing, law and order, and ideologized entertainment are the main progenitors of the new communication technologies and it is, overwhelmingly, for these purposes that the advanced systems and processes are being used. Yet, all these developments could scarcely have reached their current psychotic levels without the assistance of still another vital component in the national communications system: the mass media. The media use many forms of telecommunications in the production of their services—news, entertainment, drama, music, film—and this is crucial, they interpret for all of us why we are supposed to need the new technologies. In a conflict-of-interest situation that "boggles the mind," the print and electronic media, more often than not, are part of larger conglomerates in the new information industries. Yet, in their capacity as information providers, they instruct their readers/viewers/listeners on why massive armaments are good for everyone, why the demands of the poor (people and nations) are not to be taken seriously, and why the United States must "lead" the world.

In providing these guidelines, they treat all of us daily to belligerent and, at best, partial bulletins, some of which could be primary documentation— if we survive—for a future war crimes tribunal, hearing testimony about our media gatekeepers. An issue of the *Columbia Journalism Review,* for example, carried an excessively cautious article, which nonetheless detailed the fondness of the press for presenting nuclear war to its readers and listeners and viewers as a feasible, controllable option.[32]

In this particular account, the responsibility for nuclear war mongering is shifted to the shoulders of reporters, who are described as enamored with the jargon of Pentagon briefers. This may have helped to get the article printed, but it will not do as an explanation of why lunatic reportage of this character is published. War, even nuclear war, has become an option, to be used to hold on to a transnational empire, many components of which are becoming unstuck.

Some of the individuals who have catapulted into national prominence during the last twenty-five years, have gained attention by writing and speaking "understandingly" about dropping the bomb. The late Herman Kahn became a sought-after sage because he insisted on "thinking about the unthinkable." Henry Kissinger was brought into the Rockefeller menage because of his early fascination with bomb diplomacy.

All of this means that "the information age" is a misnomer. So too is "the communications revolution." A few advanced industrial societies are striving to assure their privileges in a revolutionary world in which at least 3 billion people no longer are accepting quietly their long-standing conditions of exploitation and servility. Information systems have been developed to maintain—albeit in new ways[33]—relationships that secure the advantages enjoyed by a small part of humanity and the disadvantages that afflict the large majority.

Consequently, it is a mistake to believe that the changes required to overcome the global, national, and local disparities in human existence will be facilitated by developing telecommunications systems. In fact, the opposite result may be expected. Existing differentials and inequities will be deepened and extended with the new instrumentation and processes, despite their loudly proclaimed and widely publicized potential benefits. Only *after* sweeping change inside dozens of nations, in which ages-old social relationships are uprooted and overturned, can the possibility of using new communication technologies for human advantage begin to be considered. It can be taken for granted, also, that the technologies applied at such a time hardly will approximate those now in use and in operation.

NOTES TO CHAPTER TWO

1. This is an appropriation of a term first employed by Dallas Smythe in a different context. Dallas Smythe, "Communications: Blindspot of Western Marxism," *Canadian Journal of Political and Social Theory,* Vol. 1, No. 3, Fall 1977, pp. 1–28.

2. Jerry L. Salvaggio, "Statement of Purpose," Edward R. Murrow Symposium, July 7, 1980.

3. Such widely different observers as E. P. Thompson, the distinguished English historian, and the Reverend Billy Graham share anxiety over the level of military spending and the amount of stockpiled weapons.

4. Hannes Alfven, "Human IQ vs. Nuclear IQ," *Bulletin of the Atomic Scientists,* January, 1981, p. 5.

5. It is reported that "The communications program is the top priority in President Reagan's recently disclosed $180 billion plan to revitalize the nation's strategic deterrent." Richard Halloran, "Reagan Arms Policy Said To Rely Heavily on Communications," The *New York Times,* October 21, 1981.

6. Simon Ramo, *America's Technology Slip,* New York, Wiley, 1980, p. 283.

7. William J. Broad, "Who Should Get the Glory for Inventing the Computer?" The *New York Times,* March 22, 1983, p. C-1.

8. Philip M. Boffey, "Three U.S. Studies Aim To Foster Advances In 'Supercomputers'," The *New York Times,* May 5, 1983.

9. "Super Computers," *Newsweek,* July 4, 1983, p. 62.

10. Marjorie Sun, "The Pentagon's Ambitious Computer Plan," *Science,* Vol. 222, December 16, 1983, pp. 1213–1215.

11. Herbert I. Schiller and Joseph D. Phillips, *Superstate: Readings In The Military-Industrial Complex,* Urbana, University of Illinois Press, 1970.

12. Steven J. Marcus, "Corporate Push for Space Lasers," The *New York Times,* April 24, 1983.

13. Annual Report To The Congress, Caspar W. Weinberger, Secretary of Defense, Fiscal Year 1984 Budget, FY 1985 Authorization Request and FY 1984–1988 Defense Program, Washington, D.C., U.S. Government Printing Office, February 1, 1983.

14. William J. Broad, "Pentagon Orders End to Computer Babel," *Science,* Vol. 211, January 2, 1981, pp. 31–33.

15. Andrew Pollack, "Military Computer Program Success," The *New York Times,* April 11, 1983.

16. Broad, *op. cit.*

17. Philip Taubman, "Choice for C.I.A. Deputy Is an Electronic-Age Spy," The *New York Times,* February 2, 1981.

18. David Burnham, "The Silent Power of the N.S.A.," The *New York Times Magazine,* March 27, 1983.

19. Brian Toohey, "How Australians Are Kept in the Dark (While the U.S. Listens In)," *National Times* (Australia), November 16–22, 1980.

20. Desmond Ball, *A Suitable Piece of Real Estate,* Sydney, Australia, Hale & Iremonger, 1980.

21. David Burnham, *op.cit* (The most comprehensive account of the National Security Agency is James Bamford's *The Puzzle Palace,* Boston, Houghton-Mifflin, 1982 and New York, Penguin, 1983.)

22. Charles Morgan, "The Spies That Hear All," *San Diego Newsline,* Vol. 4, No. 11, December 17–24, 1980. (Emphasis in text)

23. Philip Taubman, "Secrecy of U.S. Reconnaissance Office is Challenged," The *New York Times,* March 1, 1981.

24. *Ibid.*

25. Anthony G. Oettinger, "Information Resources: Knowledge and Power in the 21st Century," *Science,* Vol. 209, July 4, 1980, pp. 191–198.

26. Richard Halloran, "Military Is Divided Over Space Policy," The *New York Times,* July 5, 1983. (Emphasis added)

27. Sarah Goddard Power, *The Communications Revolution,* Current Policy No. 254, United States Department of State, Bureau of Public Affairs, Washington, D.C., Government Printing Office, December 5, 1980. (Emphasis added)

28. And these require close scrutiny as well.

29. "Why Britain Fails With the Freak Chip," The *Guardian,* April 14, 1983.

30. Herbert I. Schiller, *Who Knows: Information in the Age of the Fortune 500,* Norwood, N.J.: Ablex Publishing Corporation, 1981.

31. Cees J. Hamelink, *Cultural Autonomy In Global Communications,* New York, Longman, Inc., 1983.

32. Fred Kaplan, "Going Native Without A Field Map," *Columbia Journalism Review,* January/February, 1981, pp. 23–29.

33. Herbert I. Schiller, *Who Knows: Information in the Age of the Fortune 500,* Norwood, N.J., Ablex Publishing Coroporation, 1981.

Chapter Three

Information and the Push for Privatization and Productivity in the U.S. Economy

Twenty-five years ago, Gunnar Myrdal, an internationally reknowned Swedish social scientist, delivered the Storrs Lectures on Jurisprudence at the Yale Law School. His lectures, published two years later,[1] surveyed developments in the Western market economies. He came to some optimistic but seemingly quite reasonable conclusions.

Declaring that state intervention in the practices of the economic systems of the West was largely in response to the increasingly violent economic crises in the twentieth century, Myrdal considered that the welfare state was a progressive development. It was acting, he wrote, to protect the social and economic needs of the people. He believed that it furthered the democratization of the political process.

Additionally, Myrdal was convinced that no Western country would ever again tolerate severe unemployment. He regarded this as the crowning achievement of the welfare state. More enthusiastic still about the direction of this kind of society, Myrdal declared that "a created harmony has come to exist in the advanced Welfare State" (p. 77) and that most people feel freer in this environment (p. 86).

Recalling these views, expressed a quarter of a century ago, is not intended to denigrate a scholar whose inclinations have been humane and whose analyses often better grounded than most in the international social science community. Rather they are useful for appreciating how far thinking has moved in a different direction in the last few years.

What has been happening at an accelerating pace is the undoing of the "created harmony." A rapid dismantling is underway of the public sector that had emerged from the State's social interventions over the last one hundred years, and in the first half of this century in particular.

Myrdal's analysis calls attention also to what today would appear to be a striking paradox. According to his and others' understanding, it was the imperative of economic crisis that made necessary the interventionist state and the growth of the public sector in pre-World War II years. In the 1980s, crisis is again a central preoccupation in the West but the means of coping with it are entirely different, or so it would seem. Instead of an expansion, the public sector is being contracted. Privatization proceeds apace.[2]

What accounts for the very different means by which economic crisis is being handled today in the Western economies, especially in the United Kingdom and in the United States? It is the contention here that information and information technology play crucial, if not determining roles, in this latest stage of capitalist development and crisis.

What follows is a brief overview of the extent to which erstwhile public functions in the United States are being transferred to private, profitmaking enterprise; an explanation of why this is happening; and, finally, what already are, as well as what are likely to be, some of the effects of the push toward privatization.

UNDERCUTTING THE PUBLIC SECTOR

We do not need to be "futurists" to be able to recognize the patterns that are being established now for the years ahead. One hard-to-miss feature of the current institutional landscape is the wave of privatization sweeping over society, pushing back and often eliminating spheres of activity that historically have been public and non-commercial. Most heavily affected are the cultural, educational, health, and economic security of large groups of people.

Indigent municipal governments, for example, supplicate private companies to build or maintain their parks and other social services.[3] Shopping centers offer occasional resting places to weary shoppers but their interior malls are private enclaves, whose owners are insistent on their right to deny public access at their discretion. Financially-stricken public institutions are enabled to remain open on selected days or evenings through the largesse of private patrons—who sometimes inscribe their corporate logos in gilt letters on the entrance doors.

In St. Louis, advertising space on parking meters is being sold to raise money for the municipality.[4] Gold medallions struck by the federal government are being sold by a private company.[5] Proposals have been made to introduce Coast Guard charges for rescues at sea.[6]

The private envelopment of what was once public space and activity reaches further. Some of the most prestigious museums are establishing joint housekeeping with corporate partners. In Stamford, Connecticut, for example, a branch of the Whitney Museum has moved into the Champion International Corporation complex. The same trendsetter, the Whitney, will be opening another branch—almost like a transnational banking corporation—in the Philip Morris Corporation's new headquarters on Park Avenue in New York City.

These are admittedly small markers but there are more substantive indicators of the decline of the public sphere. Public school systems are shut down weeks or months ahead of scheduled closing because of exhausted finances. Public libraries across the country are open on a part-time basis only, and unable often to maintain even this partial service. Mass public transit in a number of major urban areas is near collapse. The public mails —about which more will be said later—are in no better shape and private delivery systems are flourishing.

Until there was an outcry from some parts of the private sector itself— from those whose interests felt threatened—the Reagan Administration proposed to sell the national weather service to private enterprise.[7]

Finally, and perhaps most important, information basic to the administration of society, is now, sometimes in the first instance, in the hands of the private corporate sector. The Director General of Sweden's Data Inspection Board, notes this development:

> Authorities in the public sector used to get their information direct from individuals. Today there are big concentrates of information serving as larder for all kinds of activities. Personnel administration and management information files are such larders. A standard system for personnel administration can hold a lot more than a hundred personal pieces of information. The employer needs only a small part of this information. Nevertheless it is gathered and included in his file in order to be handed over in due course to taxation authorities, health insurance authorities, the sheriff, trade unions, employers' organizations, statisticians who organize welfare in society and so on. *By a silent revolution—or by this new technique, if you prefer—a great part of the administration of the public sector has been moved over to the employers!*[8]

THE PUBLIC SECTOR DEFINED

These conditions would seem to describe a decaying social order on the point of breakdown. Yet it is an incomplete picture, partly because it is based on a misleading understanding of what constitutes the public sector. Also, it ignores other developments in the economy that demonstrate substantial growth and vitality.

The public sector is no monolith with a single social function. It is, in practice, a combination of operational machinery (the bureaucracy); a congeries of social functions; and, a large apparatus of coercive force. The blend, at any one time, depends on the historical moment and the contending strengths of the underlying social forces, the property-holding and the employed classes. Consequently, the public sector is an historically changing category, immediately and continuously the outcome of social struggles and politico-economic crises.

In America, capitalistic from the outset with a few exceptions in specific locales, many activities in earlier times were left to the state either because they were unprofitable to private enterprise, or, they were deemed important to the development and protection of the new nation. In some instances both reasons applied. For example, the national mails were essential for national growth but providing service to the outlying, vast continental settlements was hardly a profitable activity.

In the early decades of the Republic, it was possible and indeed likely that the growth of the nation and expanded governmental functions corresponded to the interests of the governing class. At the same time, the services that were developed were of undeniable value and comfort to the entire population. Some of these included the mails, the promotion of transportation and commerce, the extension of literacy with schools and libraries, and the establishment of municipal and state utilities.

Later along came telegraph and telephone and broadcasting. But these were private undertakings from their inception. They were regulated by the government as monopolies. Regulation of the telephone and subsequently, broadcasting, is illustrative of a public sector function that basically favored the ownership class. The regulation, more likely than not, accorded with the needs and well being of the industry. At the same time, however, the regulation did confer general utility and satisfaction: e.g., eventually, universal telephone service became an accepted standard, and broadcast programming, for which no charge was levied, also was institutionalized.

In this sense, the bureaucratic-regulatory role of government, an important constituent of the public sector, can be regarded as an ambiguous function. It is of indisputable advantage to capital, but it is also capable, under certain historical circumstances, of affording benefits to the general public, including the least advantaged groupings in the nation.

There is, however, no ambiguity about the coercive component in the public sector. As the state, from its earliest formation, is organized by and for its most powerful constituents and groupings, it is these that supervise and command the coercive instruments, the police, the armed forces, and the intelligence services. Officers holding the command posts in these services have been vetted thoroughly for their dedication and reliability to the prevailing order. This sector is public only insofar as it derives its financial support from general tax levies. The public pays for, but the governors depend on, the police and the rest of the control machinery.

There is finally, the social welfare component of the public sector. Customarily, it is this sphere which is generally considered to represent what is called the public sector. And it is true that this area comes closest to the ideal of a public sphere. It is concerned directly, to some extent, with education, health, old age, and general security.

Yet this part of the government especially is a socially determined category, representing at any one time, the historical and contemporary balance of social forces. The welfare features in this component, protestations notwithstanding, have never been fully accepted or acceptable, to the affluent governing class. Bitter battles continue to be waged in the United States and elsewhere for job security, workers' protection on the job, and for overall guarantees against the cyclical fluctuations of capitalism. It is precisely here that the current attack of capital is concentrated.

From all this, one can conclude that the public sector is a heterogeneous sphere of governmental non-profit activity, embedded in a private, capitalist economy. It is never absolute, never unchanging, and frequently ambiguous insofar as the benefits and protection it offers to the general population.

Surrounding the public sector is the corporate sphere, benignly labelled the "private sector." Though there are actually millions of private businesses in America, it is the huge corporations that account for the greatest share of the nation's production, employment, profits, and investment. A few thousand companies at most, hold the levers of national economic power, and thereby largely direct the political system. The same enterprises undertake their operations on a global scale. A majority of them derive substantial and increasing shares of their revenues from their international activity. The accretion of wealth and power in the concentrated corporate sphere in recent decades has been staggering.

INFORMATION FOR CRISIS MANAGEMENT AND THE DESTRUCTION OF THE SOCIAL COMPONENT OF THE PUBLIC SECTOR

What has happened to disrupt the "created harmony," the faint outlines of which Myrdal thought he saw and wrote about a quarter of a century ago? What forces have cut into the public sector and drained it of its social character while simultaneously promoting the growth of its coercive side? What explains the movement to privatize—turn into profit-making activities—so many functions up to recently managed by public authority and regarded as socially desirable, non-profitmaking areas?

Decisive, though not an exclusive factor in these developments, is the tremendous power, wealth, and authority of the core corporate sector, grown monstrously in the last forty years. Then, there is a reappearance of sharp economic crisis and the resulting intensifying competition between the Western European, U.S., and Japanese market economies. Lastly, and coincidental with these developments, are the invention and deployment, also since the end of the Second World War, of new information technologies and processes.

BIG BUSINESS AFTER THE WAR

The Welfare State was one of the outcomes of the great crisis and long depression of the 1930s, though its origins can be traced further back still. The American economy did not climb out of its slump until the war abroad made enormous demands on American industries for maximum output. After the war, American industries found the domestic markets of the exhausted European powers, as well as the Europeans' colonial holdings, thrown open to their exports and investments. American companies grew rapidly in the postwar boom. Their assets climbed astronomically on the profits flowing in from international and domestic demand.

While the boom based on postwar reconstruction abroad and expansion at home lasted, the corporate order could tolerate a growing social welfare sector to which it contributed, at least in part. Also, there was no urgent need to check the advances of its working force. Deals were struck which allowed organized labor in the major industries to share (modestly) in the great revenue stream that flowed into corporate treasuries. In return, organized labor supported unquestioningly, indeed enthusiastically, American foreign policy from cold war expansionism to anti-socialist interventions.

When the boom finally began to subside and markets began to become far more competitive, American corporate controllers, not surprisingly, also began to see things differently. Speedily, economic concessions were sought from the state and company obligations to social welfare were reduced to the barest minimum.

It is noted occasionally, though hardly given the attention it deserves, that the corporate income tax has practically been repealed through the practice of widespread exemptions and allowances. And while corporate strategies for withholding funds from general social services achieve striking success, other, individual property-holders, are no less adept in adopting tactics of tax avoidance. It is reported, for example, that "44 percent of all capital gains—profits on sale of securities, real estate, commodities and other forms of wealth—went unreported [to the Internal Revenue Service in 1981]."[9] And this is probably an understatement! A significant source of the public sector's economic woes, therefore, is the ability of property to determine national resource allocation to suit itself. Property-holders, especially the major corporate ones, do not contribute to national housekeeping in proportion to their ability to pay, or, to the benefits they receive.

The unwillingness of Congress to enact legislation in 1983, to insure the collection of taxes on interest and dividend income is yet another reminder of the ability of the investing class to avoid what is, for the population at large, a national legal obligation.[10]

The corporate order, besides withdrawing its economic support for the social needs of the nation, also has returned to its prewar, open and aggressive opposition to organized labor. Now, however, it possesses, along with the traditional weapons, modern means for combating labor. These include consultants, public relations, advertising, and general access to its own as well as the national informational system.

While availing itself fully of the legal, political, and modern ideological means at its disposal, American big business continues to place its greatest reliance on familiar and traditional capitalist methods to maintain profits and retain markets. To overcome crisis, according to longstanding entrepreneurial wisdom, demands ruthless cost-cutting, wages, above all, and sweeping rationalization of plant and equipment—labor displacement.

Each national market economy proceeds from these same assumptions. It is for this reason that the new information technologies and processes are seen by managers and decision-makers in all market economies, as providential means of delivery from economic slump. The new equipment and systems, according to this logic, should increase productivity, cut labor costs, and, not least, intimidate the work force so that it will accept cutbacks and "give backs."

Still according to this reasoning, labor costs throughout the economy will be lowered while entirely new lines of goods and services—computers, peripherals, programming, entertainment, etc.—can be produced. These, it is hoped, may take up some of the slack created by the continuing slump in the older industries.

Those with a more daring vision, see the new technologies as a means of reorganizing the global division of labor. In this view, the already industrialized countries will move to a new and higher rung on the international production ladder and maintain world dominance through the seizure of the information-handling machinery.[11]

There is more than mere fantasy involved here. Whether it will work itself out in the manner its promotors envision, is still an open question, but the capability of the new technologies to change significantly the means of production seems no longer an unproved assertion. Consequently, the information sphere is becoming the pivotal point in the American economy. And, as the uses of information multiply exponentially by virtue of its greatly enhanced refinement and flexibility—through computer processing, storing, retrieving, and transmitting data—*information itself becomes a primary item for sale.*

The emergence of information as a valuable good, applicable to a wide range of uses, is certainly one of the primary factors in the sweeping changes occurring in the economy. Along with the current drive of capital to cut costs and rationalize production to meet the crisis—and assisting in those objectives—information in its commodity role has become a basic determinant in the growing privatization in the economy-at-large.[12]

Activities, functions, and services that until recently were limited, relatively unchanging and unprofitable, all at once have become potential and actual profit centers with the assistance of the new information technologies. Health, education, municipal services—information itself, suddenly have emerged as sites for private investment and profit-making activity. Banking, insurance, communications, advertising, travel, and entertainment are now dependent on massive information flows and vast amounts of data processing. These are the developments that are packaged attractively in the so-called "information society."

As the possession of, or at least access to information, is now a means of profit-making, information stockpilers and stockpiles are being swept up by private enterprisers, searching out new areas for investment. On all sides, functions that rarely were regarded as revenue makers are being eyed, taken over, and reorganized with the assistance of improved information handling. This is the source of privatization in much of the economy today. It is especially visible in the information field itself, where longstanding non-profit arrangements are being pushed aside to incorporate information production, processing, and dissemination into money-making activities.

The consequences of the changing importance and growing commercialization of information are extraordinary. Once information is a saleable item, as it now is, the public institutions that customarily have produced, preserved, and disseminated it—universities, libraries, and the government itself—are themselves forced to become privatized or lose their function in the information process. Accordingly, the observable changes affecting public informational and cultural institutions across the country, to a large extent, are attributable to treating information as a commodity.

As recently as 1979, a museum director could call upon the example of libraries and universities to defend the principle of public financing. The Director of the Cleveland Museum of Art, for example, declared that museums "should be like libraries and universities and get their money with as few strings attached as possible."[13]

This is no longer either an appropriate comparison or recommendation. Those units of the nation's universities which are sources of potentially profitable information—micro-biology, micro-electronics, artificial intelligence, etc.—are being integrated, financially or structurally, with corporate enterprise. In March 1982, for example, a private meeting (the public and the press were excluded) brought together the "presidents of five major universities with the leaders of ten high-technology companies and a group of prominent scientists. . .to try to work out guidelines to govern the growing commercialization of scientific research, especially in biotechnology."[14]

Science magazine reported that the Pajaro Dunes Conference—named after the meeting site—was unable to resolve such issues as the exclusive rights that industry secures from the university research it sponsors.[15] The search for agreement continues.

Meanwhile, the national laboratories of the Federal Government are being forced to yield to the same influence. There are 755 laboratories in the federal system "ranging from tiny facilities with a handful of employees to enormous installations the size of small towns."[16] The budget for these laboratories in fiscal 1984 is more than 15 billion dollars and the research carried out is on military, energy, health, space, and agricultural problems.

Business Week reports that "the labs are opening themselves to industry. More and more companies from Exxon Corp. to 3M Co., are enthusiastically forging collaborative ties with the labs on projects..."[17]

The account notes further that in the past, the main obstacle to industry collaborating with the labs was "the difficulty of conducting proprietary research," that is, keeping the research findings private for company commercial utilization and application.

This barrier has been swept away and the road is clear for the largest corporations to do just that. As current "partners" with various federal laboratories, *Business Week* lists, among others, Dupont, Exxon, 3M, Bell Labs, Gulf, IBM, Xerox, Rockwell, Allied Chemical, Hewlett-Packard, Ford, Babcock and Wilcox, Westinghouse, and GM.

"Many in government," *Business Week* adds, "find it difficult to justify granting exclusive patent licenses for work conducted at the taxpayers' expense."

Troubling to some or not, the private appropriation of public property has become the general pattern and it is being applied to the entire information generating sector. It is not only universities and governmental labs that are beginning to be enmeshed in a widening net of commercial enterprise.

Public and university libraries are experiencing similar pressures from the pull and tug of private information suppliers and vendors. Holdings and acquisitions are being put into machine readable formats, while libraries themselves are being obliged to link up their facilities with the data bases offered by commercial vendors—Lockheed, System Development Corporation, Bibliographic Retrieval Service, etc.

Library information capability undeniably is greatly enhanced. Yet this benefit is accompanied by the abandonment of libraries' historical free access policy. User charges are introduced. The public character of the library is weakening as its commercial connection deepens. No less important, the composition and character of its holdings change as the clientele shifts from the general public to the ability-to-pay user.[18]

Similar powerful forces are at work in the nation's largest storehouse of publicly-generated information, the national government's information supply. Increasingly, the heavy output and great holdings of scientific and social information of the federal government are being organized, packaged, and sold by private information companies. "Those who rely on free or reduced-price information published by the government," reports the *National Journal,* "are finding that it is becoming more difficult and sometimes impossible to obtain."[19]

Information which was produced originally from the expenditures of public funds is being acquired by private information companies for commercial sale. The privatization of the governmental information supply is a complex process which includes the transfer of public data to corporate ownership and a combination of policies that are reducing or eliminating full public access to publicly-compiled information.[20] The Information Industry Association (IIA) wages a relentless campaign on behalf of private information vendors and packagers against public preparation and dissemination of governmentally-acquired information.[21]

The privatization of public information in the governmental sector is undertaken with careful semantic protection. "In a relatively short time," a library publication notes, "the phrase 'national information policy' has had its meaning drastically narrowed from designation of the collective needs and rights of all Americans to a kind of code word expressing the concerns of the private sector, and especially its claims to the riches it perceives in the bureaucratic wilderness preserves of government-produced and distributed information."[22]

COMMERCIALIZATION AND PRIVATIZATION OF THE FIRST AMENDMENT

The new information technology, in addition to being used to create an ability-to-pay standard for information which used to be socially available, facilitates the privatization of information and human values in still more direct ways. The flexibility and penetrability of the new instrumentation, and the greatly expanded number of channels available for message transmission, enable non-media corporations—enterprises whose main economic activity is *not* media production—to engage heavily in message making and dissemination.

The television production facilities at the disposal of the big, non-media firms already surpass the installations owned by the commercial national media networks.[23] The outpouring of corporate messages, directly to general publics is still at an early stage but already it is considerable. Cable TV and video cassettes are favored means of distribution. Programs for in-plant audiences ordinarily are transmitted through closed-circuit systems. But much of this corporate media production is offered without cost to commercial outlets and may be played in entirety or in part, often without attribution to the original producer.

Some suggestion of the possible greatly enhanced future significance of private corporate media outputs are the rulings of the Supreme Court in recent years. In one important case in 1978, the Court ruled that "corporate speech" is entitled to the same protection as individual speech under the First Amendment.[24] In this startling, but not inconsistent with earlier interpretation(s), the Bill of Rights is made an accomplice of privatization and corporate power.

IDEOLOGICAL PRIVATIZATION: ADVERTISING

Alongside these new forms of private message creation and dissemination, there is the ongoing and continuously expanding volume of commercial advertising, penetrating deeper and extinguishing further what remains of individual and public space.

For decades, the United States has had the dubious distinction of leadership of the world in advertising expenditures, calculated either absolutely or on a per capita basis. With the growth of the transnational corporation, many nations are being elevated—if that is the appropriate way of putting it —to the American level.

The development of direct satellite broadcasting—signals from a communication satellite beamed directly into a home receiver without passing through an intermediary—produces euphoria in the advertising community. The chairman of J. Walter Thompson (Britain), one of the top ten transnational ad agencies, has this vision of the future for pan-European television:

> For the first time, it would seem, we can fulfill the multinational's corporate dream: to establish at a single moment in time, eyeball to eyeball interface with the man in the street on a global scale. What power, what savings, what consistency, what an opportunity![25]

To those who thought the point of saturation had been reached in the United States, the projections of the advertising industry for the next twenty years and into the 21st century, indicate how mistaken they are. A tidal wave of commercialization, if the industry's expectations are to be taken at face value, is still to come.[26]

It seems to be so. Advertising outlays, in all media, rise from year to year. Though difficult to prove empirically, the impact of the flood of commercial messages on human values and behavior, should not be underestimated. How much they contribute to the reinforcement and extension of already powerful patterns of individual acquisitive and consumerist behavior cannot be specified. What is clear is that the weakening of publicly supported cultural activity proceeds apace with minimal opposition.

Internationally, the same pressures are evident and public systems of broadcasting in Europe and elsewhere are being weakened and diminished. Publicly financed systems are unable to withstand the assault of corporate-financed, advertising-supported media corporations.

EFFECTS OF PRIVATIZATION

In sum, the massive privatization of the public sector, and especially its cultural/communications component, is the outgrowth of a combination of factors at work over recent decades. There is, to begin with, the enormously expanded wealth and power of corporate business in America and in a few other advanced industrialized countries. Multibillion dollar transnational companies utilize the media and communication circuits for their direct and indirect messages. They saturate the commercial information systems of the world, while at the same time, manufacturing in-house, greatly growing numbers of messages.

The phenomenal growth of the transnational system is facilitated by the development of new information technologies which allow the tight coordination of transnational global operations. Additionally, the new instrumentation and processes provide expanded opportunities for profit-making in the system overall, particularly in the field of information generation and data processing and dissemination. No less important, the new technologies are utilized increasingly in the entire production system to rationalize, cut costs, increase worker productivity, and, intentionally or not, to decrease worker autonomy.

Under these powerful systemic forces, the public domain shrinks, its activities and functions increasingly relocated in the profit-making private sector.

Does it matter?

If basic social functions are being performed, sometimes even more comprehensively with the new machinery and techniques, does it make any difference where the support comes from and how it is delivered? Does the source of the financing affect the product/service? Is there anything *inherently* harmful in the shift from public to privately-paid-for or assisted communication, education, and community services?

Some direct economic effects are immediately detectable. When information becomes exclusively a commercial product, it is information that is produced for profit. Who can pay for it and how much it will cost are questions that affect everyone. When an ability-to-pay criterion becomes the standard for information access—which is precisely what occurs when information provision and dissemination are turned over to market enterprises—the divisions in the society deepen. The poor become poorer still because they are excluded from the means by which their condition could be improved. The rich become more affluent than ever because they have the means whereby to consolidate and extend their power base.

Some of these developments are already evident. A local situation, for example, that has its national and international analogues, is reported: "In Computer Education, Rich Districts Get Richer."[27] Another example is government information, produced with public money, turned over to private information handlers and providers. These then make the processed data available but often at prices far beyond the reach of ordinary people. A report, for example, on federal spending for information technology in 1983, using government statistics but produced by a private research firm, bore a $995 price tag.[28] And this is no longer regarded as astonishing.

Other examples abound. As the public mail service yields more and more of its functions to private businesses, the losers are the groups who cannot pay for the high-class private services—the rural communities, inner-city neighborhoods, and small suburbs.[29]

Similarly, as the national telephone system is "deregulated" and is withdrawn from public accountability, local telephone rates escalate and the end may be in sight for a universal telephone service standard. Again, library user fees are becoming standard as libraries are compelled to computerize and tie into privately-owned data banks. Finally, universities that link up with the high tech private sector overcome the funding troubles of those schools left out. In the dynamic developed in this increasingly popular relationship, courses, curricula, and research supporting the association of business and academia are privileged. Faculties that are outside the university-industrial nexus begin to resemble a proletarian work force in higher education.

These *economic* consequences of privatization of the cultural/information sphere of the public sector are only beginning to be experienced. Still it is apparent that national social divisions are being widened and hardened. The *social* damage resulting from privatization of the information sector, surprisingly enough, may be deeper still and longer lasting, though extremely difficult to measure precisely.

Once withdrawn from its social context and made into an item for sale, necessary information may just not be available. This would occur not because of censorship, though this is no small concern, but for the reason that it will be controlled by the marketplace. Information we should have or might need may never be gathered, much less organized and transmitted. If it is produced, it will have to be purchased. With the destruction of public information, the basis of democracy disappears.

There are still other perils inherent in an information/cultural order administered and financed largely by a few thousand super corporations. One is that a people's social consciousness is made the prime target for ideological attack.

A recent study, generally favorable to corporate philanthropy in education and the arts, suggests the direction that may be expected in such an order. The question is asked: "Should Business Support Those Who Don't Support The System?" The reply:

> Corporations have no obligations to provide funds to organizations or individuals that are devoted to the replacement of our economic, political and social system by some other system. This would be foolhardy. Looking at it from another viewpoint, it is appropriate for corporations to provide support to worthwhile organizations that are proponents of the free enterprise system ...On the other hand, it is unwise for corporations to fund those who, while well motivated, would damage or destroy the system they nominally support with reforms that are unworkable or unnecessary.[30]

There is evidence enough to conclude that this is precisely the outlook of prevailing corporate authority. Gulf Oil, one of the patrons of public television, for example, calls attention to the programming it supports with newspaper and magazine headlines such as these: "We Believe Television Should Command Your Attention," and "We Believe Television Should Explore Vast Wastelands. Not Be One." To generate what it terms "provocative" programming, Gulf collaborates with the National Geographic Society and offers the viewing public such items as *"Polar Bear Alert,"* "The Thames," the world of wild chimpanzees, and efforts to save the whooping cranes, an endangered species.

All of these themes are surely unobjectionable and hardly ideological—except, insofar as they are presented as provocative material and actually preempt time and resources that could be applied to genuinely thought provoking work.

In the same vein, Mobil, also a benefactor of public television and other cultural projects, found it necessary to request the return of its contribution, a sum of $1000, to the American Writers' Congress, in the Fall of 1981. According to Mobil's Robert P. Maxon:

> The meeting was not directed at preserving the character and quality of our literary culture—it was a political platform to advance causes contrary to the fundamental ideals upon which America is based. The political positions taken by the Congress are an anathema, and we disavow any association with them...[31]

The record could be added to at will. The decisive issue is not overt censorship by corporate free enterprise bluenoses, though of course, this occurs regularly. It is rather the creation of a cultural-communications atmosphere in which the dialogue is purged at the outset of critical discourse and of significant, alternative formulations. Self-censorship becomes a built-in component in intellectual and creative work. Eventually, it enters into the mode of social existence.

This is the *production* side of the process. On the *consumption* side, that of the national public, impacts are no less great, and no less easily measurable. Navigating in a media-pervasive environment, almost all of which is commercially-saturated, the viewer/listener/reader is suffused with corporate ideology and is instructed day and night on the benefits of privatized behavior.

One prominent corporate supporter of the arts emphasizes that "bringing the arts to the people is the core of the capitalist system."[32] Perhaps! More persuasive is the acknowledged corporate effort to create for itself an aura of social responsibility and good citizenship by contributing to national cultural activity. David Rockefeller, in 1966, calling for a much larger role for business corporations in the arts, put it this way:

> It can provide a company with extensive publicity and advertising, a brighter public reputation, and an improved corporate image. It can build better customer relations, a readier acceptance of company products, and a superior appraisal of their quality. Promotion of the arts can improve the morale of employees and help attract qualified personnel.[33]

Philip Morris Corporation, a major contributor to the nation's health problem, as well as a generator of cultural pollution with its advertising, at least has a forthright Board Chairman. He has said: "We are in an unpopular industry. [While] our support of the arts is not directed toward that [problem], it has given us a better image in the financial and general community than had we not done this."[34]

IBM's art benefactions are considered a "great insurance policy." And few failed to miss the greatly increased support from the "seven sisters" who dominate the international oil industry, for public TV and related cultural events that coincided with the price-gouging and profit-taking accompanying the oil crisis in the 1970s.

Still, these initiatives are all well within familiar traditions of the American historical experience. What make the current practices and institutional changes unique and especially dangerous are, they are deepening, at an alarming rate, the gulf between popular understanding and global realities.

An increasing number of Americans are being informed, educated, and entertained by corporate-created or sponsored media and cultural programs and materials that exclude or minimize or misrepresent the great social conflicts of our time and the near global insistence on fundamental change in economic and cultural relationships.

In this process, the informational apparatus, the arts, and the educational enterprise are being locked into supporting, or at least not confronting critically, a system of transnational business and culture which is coming under scrutiny and challenge almost everywhere else around the world. Communications and creativity in America, in sharp contrast, are being identified positively with corporate production and management.

The many ways in which the information structure and the creative material that passes through it are being utilized and linked directly to the private sector, may be of assistance in the near term in relieving pressure and diverting attention from the social issues that trouble people everywhere. In the long-term, the efforts and outputs of the privatized cultural communications sphere will lose their credibility by their unwillingness or inability to illuminate the problems that Americans and everyone else are affected by. But the dangers are present now and non-deferrable.

For a very long time, we have known but not admitted that what is needed desperately in the country, is an expansion, actually an explosion, of *human* services: educational, health, cultural, social, etc. It is a feat of a disordered imagination to see these created in a *private* context. Human services are the quintessential *social* expressions of community.

The facts that medical and health services are now produced increasingly by privately owned and administered systems and that there are chains of for-profit hospitals, are startling indicators of how far privatization has entered into the fabric of American life.[35]

Yet it is the private envelopment of the communication-cultural sector that severely limits, practically excludes, public knowledgability and open debate of these developments. The agendas of the major political parties avoid these subjects. Public discussion, for the most part, is nonexistent. The proposals for coping with the current, still relatively manageable economic crisis—leaving aside the crises looming—are pathetic in their narrow vision. The most elementary and basic questions of political economy are ignored for fear of contradicting the tenets of privatism. Perhaps social solutions hardly can be expected to be formulated, much less implemented, when people have been systematically privatized in their physical, spiritual, spatial, and cultural lives.

But while privatization accelerates, so do the social breakdowns, at home and abroad. These intrude despite considerable efforts to contain and screen them out of popular awareness. For the fact of the matter is, the private sector, comprised of divergent interests, is unable to administer, much less coordinate, the national economy, especially in a period of increasing general turbulence.

The situation already has become bizarre. There is a crumbling public sector with dispirited supporters, under siege from a private sector, which is itself in continuous battle among its own groupings. Actually, the antagonistic and conflictive activity *inside* the private corporate sector, limits for the moment, at least, the full force of privatization from being experienced throughout the social realm.

Whether private sector internal disagreements can be relied upon to protect the common interest in the long-term, is quite another matter. The pressure of intensifying economic and social crisis more likely will compel the beleaguered system to find increasing attraction in a "command economy," in which the orders come from the most powerful private commanders. In this connection, it is of interest that privatization has not overtaken the coercive side of the public sector. Despite an obsession with cost reductions in the social sphere, it is reported that "Since President Reagan took office in 1981, the department [of Justice] has gained a 43 percent budget increase, excluding the new request [for 1985]."

The Assistant Attorney General for Administration explained this happy state of the Department: "...now there is a recognition of Justice, as the agency that delivers domestic defense."[36] And so it does. The moneys appropriated so generously go for expanding the FBI, enlarging the prison system, and acquiring the most up-to-date technologies for lawyers and investigators.[37]

If indeed, this is the direction in which affairs go, the communication/cultural sphere would be one of the first areas of attention and *direct* intervention. Signs of this are already evident in the many information restrictions being imposed by the executive branch of the government.[38]

It is moving to the rim of the abyss to put hope in the intensification of crisis. But it seems there are few, if any, alternatives. The sense and pursuit of community have been so badly undermined that their recapture requires a momentous reversal in social-political direction. In the years immediately ahead this seems doubtful.

The special lesson that the Thatcher government in Britain provides, is that even a stricken advanced capitalism still possesses a great capacity to smother its opposition, divert and disorient popular resistance, and, push back living standards of the weaker sectors of society to pre-World War II levels.

Under what and whose auspices an alternative reconstitution of our own social order will occur, if indeed it does, are at this time unknown and perhaps unpredictable.

NOTES TO CHAPTER THREE

1. Gunnar Myrdal, *Beyond the Welfare State,* New Haven, Yale University Press, 1960.
2. In 1982, President Reagan signed Executive Order 12369, establishing the President's Private Sector Survey on Cost Control. An Executive Committee

under J. Peter Grace, assembled a task force of 161 high-level private sector executives to carry out the assignment. In September 1983, the Committee reported its findings to the President, in a document titled "Report on Privatization" (U.S. Government Printing Office, Washington, D.C. 1983). The Report is a paean to privatization, which it defines as follows:

> "Privatization, in a literal sense, means to turn over an activity, or part of an activity, currently performed by the Federal Government to a non-Federal entity. It is an option for implementing Government programs and policies, allowing the Government to *provide* services without *producing them*." (Emphasis in text)

3. The *New York Times,* April 1, 1982.

4. The *New York Times,* June 25, 1983.

5. The *New York Times,* April 13, 1983.

6. The *New York Times,* April 24, 1983.

7. "A Government That Would Sell the Sky," The *New York Times,* May 14, 1983.

8. Jan Freese, "The Right To Be Alone in Sweden," *TDR* (Transnational Data Report), Vol. VI, No. 8, December, 1983, p. 477 (Emphasis added).

9. Edward Cowan, "Dole Bill To Ask Brokers to File Gains by Clients," The *New York Times,* March 6, 1982.

10. "Congress Passes Repeal of Interest Withholding," The *New York Times,* July 29, 1983.

11. John M. Eger, "The International Information War," *Computerworld,* Vol. 15, No. 11a, March 18, 1981.

12. Some see other explanations for the shift to privatization. Hirschman suggests a non-material factor. In his reading of history as well as recent developments, he regards the shift from public to private involvements essentially occurring as the result of *disappointment.* The high expectations that individuals had for public sector activities were not fulfilled. In reaction, there is a pronounced turn to private sector preoccupations. The changes are expressed in terms of individual preferences and subjective valuations. A. D. Hirschman, *Shifting Involvements, Private Interest and Public Action,* Princeton, Princeton University Press, 1982.

13. Robert Metz, "The Corporation As Art Patron: a Growth Stock," *Art News,* May, 1979.

14. Fox Butterfield, "Town and Gown of High Tech Seeking Guidelines," The *New York Times,* March 25, 1982.

15. Barbara J. Culliton, "Pajaro Dunes: The Search for Consensus," *Science,* Vol. 216, 1982, pp. 155–158.

16. Philip M. Boffey, "Experts Criticize U.S. Laboratories for Deficiencies," The *New York Times,* July 16, 1983.

17. "Industry Finds a New Ally in the National Labs," *Business Week,* April 18, 1983, pp. 44E–44K.

18. Anita R. Schiller, "Instruction or Information: What's Changed?" The *Reference Librarian,* Vols. 1 & 2, Fall/Winter 1981.
19. The *National Journal,* August 6, 1983.
20. Anita R. Schiller and Herbert I. Schiller, "The Privatizing of Information: Who Can Own What America Knows?" The *Nation,* April 7, 1982, pp. 461–463.
21. Jake Kirchner, "IIA Statement Calls for Reliance on Private Sector," *Computerworld,* September 5, 1983, p. 1.
22. *LJ/SLJ Hotline,* Vol. XI, No. 12, March 29, 1982, p. 5.
23. Sol Hurwitz, "On the Road to Wired City," *Harvard Magazine,* September/October, 1979, pp. 18–19.
24. *First National Bank of Boston, et al.* vs. *Bellotti,* 435 U.S. 765 (1978).
25. E. Newman, "European States Face Problem of Controlling Their Neighbors' TV," *Wall Street Journal,* March 22, 1982.
26. Robert J. Coen, "Vast U.S. and Worldwide Ad Expenditures Expected," *Advertising Age,* November 13, 1980, pp. 1–16.
27. M. Winerip, "In Computer Education, Rich Districts Get Richer," The *New York Times,* June 24, 1983.
28. *Computerworld,* September 19, 1983.
29. Joseph A. Califano, "The Little Guy Will Get Hurt," The *New York Times,* April 17, 1983.
30. F. Koch, *The New Corporate Philanthropy,* New York, Plenum Press, 1979, p. 131.
31. "Mobil Has Second Thoughts About Writers Congress," *Publishers Weekly,* Vol. 221, No. 5, January 29, 1982, p. 22.
32. R. P. Hanes, *Art News,* May, 1979, p. 61.
33. Koch, *op. cit.*
34. Metz, *op cit.*
35. Fox Butterfield, "Proposed Sale of a Hospital by Harvard Is Raising Fears," The *New York Times,* September 4, 1983; *See also,* Paul Starr, *Social Transformation of American Medicine,* New York, Basic Books, 1983.
36. L. M. Werner, "Reagan Plans Bigger Budget for U.S. Law Enforcement," The *New York Times,* January 2, 1984.
37. *Ibid.*
38. "Less Access to Less Information By and About the Government: III, A 1982–1983 Chronology," *American Library Association Washington Newsletter,* Vol. 35, No. 12, December 30, 1983.

Chapter Four

The Developing Crisis in the Western Free Flow of Information Doctrine

Industrial crisis, domestic and international, is the "environment" in which the new information technologies are being invented and deployed. Their employment is designed to overcome, or, at the very least, alleviate crisis.

This is the meaning of the mad scramble into electronics, the push toward privatization in the economy at large, the reverence for computerization, however mindless, and the obscene outlays for military communication hardware and systems to subdue an insurgent world.

Yet a crisis of another sort is looming. This crisis arises from the way the new instrumentation and systems are being managed internationally. It relates to the availability and utilization of international communication circuits as well as the character of the data and messages that flow through them. In a nutshell, the information flows that are serving the transnational business system are becoming, in themselves, a center of controversy.

Accordingly, set out below is a review of the importance of the new technologies to the international business system; the range of conflicts that could lead to the destabilization of the prevailing system of domination and control; and, an account and appraisal of recent United States policy intended to cope with the growing problem area of free flow.

RELIANCE OF THE TRANSNATIONAL CORPORATE BUSINESS SYSTEM ON THE NEW INFORMATION TECHNOLOGIES AND THE INFORMATION FLOWS THEY MAKE POSSIBLE

It has become apparent that international information flows, and the problems attendant on them, have become central concerns of those who are entrusted with the destinies of the transnational corporate order.

The Under Secretary of State for Security Assistance, Science and Technology, for example, states flatly:

For the United States, communications and information technologies are crucial. The U.S. has been the principal source and user of many of the new technologies and associated services. It has been the economic base for the ongoing communications and information revolution and through various means has made available technologies and services around the globe.[1]

More specific still, Mark Fowler, the Chairman of the Federal Communications Commission (FCC), testifying before a Congressional committee in September 1981, described developments this way:

International telecommunications is a dynamic field with an annual growth rate of at least twenty-five percent—or approximately three times that of domestic communications. The technology is advancing quickly, and this rapid growth strains the ability of the policy maker to find appropriate solutions to the institutional and substantive issues created. The single most important point to be made about international communications is that it cannot be considered in a static limited way. Further, it has become an important expression of the posture of the United States toward the rest of the world, a significant aspect of our foreign policy, and a vital tool in the economic interdependence which is becoming a fact of life for all international policy. The commission realizes that international telecommunications policy is closely aligned to certain political and economic issues, to technology transfer, and to national security matters. As many have observed, the United States is moving beyond an industrial society to an informational society, and telecommunications is the basic instrument by which this transformation is being accomplished. Questions of information flow are taking on a new importance in the business of international relations. Thus, the Commission's involvement in international telecommunications reflects its emphasis on this emerging and important area.[2]

FCC Chairman Fowler's statement touches on some of the many problems facing the directors of the U.S. transnational corporate economy. They may be summed up in one general proposition; how to maintain, or at least prevent further slippage, of U.S. hegemony in a world of increasing challenge to that domination. It is especially notable that at each pressure point identified by the FCC chairman, a communications issue is present. Information and the communications process have become the pivots of present and future national and international power relationships.[3]

The information sector is perceived and intended to serve as the springboard for the revitalization of United States capitalism, domestically and internationally. W. Michael Blumenthal, former Secretary of the Treasury in the Carter Administration, now Chairman of the Burroughs Corporation —a major producer of information handling equipment—told a National Computer Conference in the Spring of 1981:

Our urban centers have become, to a great extent, information processors and communicators...information has finally made it to center stage. Perhaps one of the seminal contributions of the 20th century to the development of the human race will be the perception and use of information as the central process around which all else revolves, the focal point of all our activities...the information industry is the fundamental force behind global interdependence.[4]

INFORMATION FLOWS FOR THE PRODUCTION OF GOODS AND SERVICES

How the new technologies, and the information flows they make possible, now contribute to the happy global state that Blumenthal terms "interdependence," is seen best in the phenomenon of "transborder data flows."

Transborder data flows (TDF) have not yet become as well known as Kleenex or Coca Cola but they are beginning to receive increasing public visibility. What precisely are these flows? Who is making them? How do they differ from what went before? Why are they in the news? What is their general significance? These are questions which address the fundamentals of the now prevailing international economy.

According to a study made by the United Nations Centre on Transnational Corporations, transborder data flows:

> ...are movements across national boundaries, of machine-readable data for processing, storage, or retrieval. 'Data' are symbols that can be handled and transmitted through computers; 'information' is the combination of data into messages intelligible to human beings; the processed form of the raw data. Such movements can be effected by nonelectronic means, e.g., on magnetic tapes, discs, punched cards, or other media. Increasingly, however, electronic means are used, which presuppose the availability of a telecommunications infrastructure. In a narrower sense, therefore, transborder data flows take place through transnational computer-communications systems. These are arrangements whereby one or several sophisticated computers in other countries are linked to affiliated computers in other countries and through them (or directly) to remote terminals. The trend in transborder data flows is towards the usage of transnational computer-communications systems...Transborder data flows involve the point-to-point delivery of messages.[5]

What distinguishes earlier international communications from that now designated as transborder data flows are the volume and the means of transmission. The amount of data currently moving internationally is enormous and the rate of growth of this kind of information traffic is accelerating. The means by which the greatest portion of these flows are transmitted are electronic, not surface transport, as in the past.

The activities of one American transnational company are illustrative:

> All *American Express* business-insurance, payment systems, asset manage-
> ment, international banking and securities—could not function without rapid,
> reliable global communications. In 1981, for example, company on-line sys-
> tems:
>
> —processed 310 million American Express Card transactions and 360 million
> Visa and Master Card transactions;
> —authorized daily 250,000 of those transactions from throughout the world
> within an average response time of five seconds;
> —processed more than 350 million American Express Travelers Cheques sold
> by more than 100,000 banks and other selling outlets around the world;
> —completed 56 million insurance premiums and claim transactions;
> —automatically executed approximately $10 billion a day in international
> banking transactions...
>
> Overall, company technical resources encompass nine major information pro-
> cessing centers, six worldwide data and time sharing network groups, 70 large
> computer systems and 229 smaller computer systems for a combined process-
> ing capacity of 170 million instructions per second.[6]

Clearly, transborder data flows have become the life support elements in
the world business system, yet it is remarkable how little is known about
them. Though there are indirect ways to estimate the approximate volume
of the data flows, detailed information about the senders and the receivers
as well as the categories of content, up to this time at least, is in extremely
short supply. This, it should be emphasized, is not because of problems of
measurement, though some of these do exist. It is the consequence of a deliberate decision to withhold information.[7]

THE NEW INTERNATIONAL DIVISION OF LABOR

The efforts devoted to keeping TDF study an empirical vacuum go well
beyond ordinary corporate concern with industrial espionage. It is an attempt to conceal from public view the true dimensions and consequences of
the farreaching transformation in the character, location of, and the controlling influences over the global production of goods and services.

Most significant in these massive changes, is the ever increasing concentration of capital and its transnationalization. What this means, in brief, is
the organization of production on a global scale under the centralized direction of powerful private companies. The establishment of operational units
in more than one country is capital's means of expansion and accumulation
beyond the confines of the national state. In seeking either a cheap and

pliant labor supply or access to new markets, or the ease of operating in weak and vulnerable societies, or all of these, and additional motivations as well, private corporations domiciled in one state become transnational entities, with facilities sometimes in dozens of different national locales.

This creates, among many other outcomes, a curious confusion over the very nature of international relationships. In international organizations such as the United Nations or the International Telecommunications Union, the relationships are between nations. Yet in the daily flow of events, *inside countries,* the decisive relationships are likely to be between transnational companies and the host state. This is a point that is stressed by several Latin American informatics leaders.

Datamation asked these questions:

> What is the role of technologically advanced countries in the development of informatics in Latin American nations? How could North-South relationships be improved?

Speaking for his own nation as well as the other states present (Mexico, Brazil, and Argentina), the Chilean president of ECON, the national computer company, replied:

> I think that the question should be reformulated because at the moment the role of the developed countries is in the hands of the multinational companies. That is to say, it is not the country that plays the role, but rather the multinational company operating in our countries that play the role.[8]

Since 1945, the largest American firms have set up branches and affiliates on all continents and in most countries. The capability to manage a globally-dispersed enterprise depends completely on information flows—voluminous, rapid, and secure. Developments in information technology have attended to these needs. Computer-satellite links have provided a vital infrastructure for corporate global business.

Without exaggeration, some industries could not operate, lacking the new information instrumentation. Banking, insurance, air transport, and travel, in general, would be unthinkable without their sophisticated communications networks. The vice-president and counsel of Continental Illinois Bank, one of the big U.S. commercial banks, gave this description of his bank's dependence on international information flows to a Congressional Committee in 1980:

> As an international bank, our business is entirely dependent upon the free flow of instantaneous communications. In the course of our banking business, we need to have minute-by-minute intelligence from the money market across the world...

In Europe, our branches enter all of their transactions into intelligent data ter-
minals which transmit this information over leased lines to Continental Bank's
communications centers in Brussels, Belgium. The data, after being assembled
and verified, is cued for high-speed data transmission to the central processing
center in Chicago; customer accounts and the bank's general ledgers are up-
dated; management reports are created, customers statements are produced;
and the processed information is then sent back to Europe for use by those
units the following business day.[9]

In addition to these important service sectors of the American economy,
a new group of information activities have come into existence in recent
years—production and service—that generate, process, transmit, store, retrieve, and disseminate information for a variety of specialized users. Manufacturers of satellites, computers, and peripheral equipment, along with
data processing companies, data bank producers and transmitters, and soft-
ware/hardware firms now constitute a large and growing component of the
total national economic activity of the U.S. economy. This is the core of the
so-called "information economy." The size of this component already
represents a significant share of U.S. corporate international economic activity. In the sphere of data processing alone, U.S. companies now handle
80 percent of world data processing.[10]

The information sector also has become indispensable to the rest of the
industrial economy. It is the supplier of the computer-directed machinery
and instrumentation that is being installed in plants across the country and
thereby becoming the basis of most production.

In the United States, and a few other already industrialized states, these
developments are evident in the gradual disappearance of the older kinds of
production, the shutdown of "smokestack" industries and the great growth
in what is called the "high tech" fields, all of which are heavy information
processors and users. This has its international dimension as well.

What is, in fact, happening at a quickening tempo, is a shift of the kind
of economic activities that are undertaken in different regions of the world.
The changing international division of labor, which is what this shift amounts
to, is not being effected according to a global plan or a specifically drafted
design. It is proceeding rather under the impetus of countless initiatives,
state and private, international and local, with the chief decision-makers
and influence wielders being the transnational corporations. These firms are
striving to broaden, facilitate, and secure their operations in one area after
another.

American Express Company's vice-president, Harry Freeman, sums up
the changing international division of labor in one sentence:

If we in the post-industrial West are to allow Brazilian steel and South Korean
shoes to penetrate our market, our dynamic service industries must in turn be

allowed to compete in world markets without unfair and burdensome restrictions.[11]

Freeman does not mention that "Brazilian steel" or "South Korean shoes" may be produced in branch plants of U.S.-owned transnational companies.

INFORMATION FLOWS FOR MARKETING AND CONSUMPTION

Without the new technologies and the information flows they facilitate, the global *production* operations of the transnational corporations would be difficult if not impossible to sustain. Still, however important, they constitute but a part of the overall economic process. *Marketing* the goods and services is the equally essential second step in the commercial transaction. Here also, information flows are indispensable.

Transnational advertising and marketing activities are predicated on the fullest access to the national media systems wherever the corporations have a foothold. In recent decades outlays by transnational advertisers have rocketed. Most of the transnational marketing messages continue to be transmitted through national channels. However, satellite transmissions, and soon, direct satellite broadcasting (DBS), may be expected to be heavily utilized by transnational advertisers.

In 1980, Robert J. Coen, a senior vice-president of the transnational advertising agency, McCann-Erickson, and regarded as "the keeper of the records of advertising expenditure," predicted that advertising expenditures world-wide, in 20 years, would reach about $800 billion, a seven-fold increase over the amount spent in 1980. The U.S. would remain the world leader by far but would drop below its current position of accounting for more than half of the world expenditures on advertising. The estimates by Coen are probably obsolete already. In any case they do not take into account an inflation factor that certainly will push the outlay figure for 2000 A.D. much higher, *assuming no major interferences* in the world political economy—a breathtaking assumption!

Coen is prepared to make this assumption and observes that:

the rest of the world is rapidly emulating many of our advertising practices and by the year 2000 these will be the norm in a number of other countries around the world. In this sense the U.S. may be considered to be a leading indicator of the developments that lie ahead in other parts of the world.[12]

One of the principal reasons why American advertising is becoming the "norm" in many countries is because it is being promoted heavily to be just that. The evolution in the broadcasting systems of many European nations, and countries elsewhere, demonstrates this. State broadcasting authorities are being weakened and sometimes replaced, or compelled to share influence with commercial entities. These are introduced or created with the support, political and financial, of the transnationals. Beside moneymaking, the objective of the commercial systems is to overcome the historical reluctance of state broadcasting authorities to permit advertising.

The need of the transnational companies to reach national audiences with their marketing messages, requires *unrestricted* access to the national media. Commercialization of broadcasting enables this to occur. Once the broadcasting system has been withdrawn from public administration, only the transnational companies have the resources to pay the substantial advertising rates. And so it has gone, from place to place.

The Italian situation is exemplary. The *International Herald Tribune* carried this report in 1982:

> Networks, Italian-style, are the latest development in Italy's commercial television boom, which has put government-run broadcasting on the defensive and created a $90 million a year market for American entertainment. . . . This bid for fully independent [commercial] network television is being closely watched in France, Spain and other European countries debating the future of official broadcasting control.[13]

Accompanying the spread of transnational corporate advertising is a new pattern of daily living, connected to the products and services heavily promoted. Under the siege of consumerist promotions, national development plans that emphasize other priorities as well as stressing social equity, are forced to recede and yield place.

How far-reaching this process can be and how it can escape national control once it has become incorporated into the institutional setting, is suggested in the following account of nutritional changes in the Mexican diet:

> Processed foods are now a staple in the Mexican diet, replacing cheaper and more nutritious traditional foods such as corn and beans. This shift in eating habits over the past 15 years has sparked concern among government and private food experts, who say that choices about what food to eat are increasingly influenced more by advertising than nutritional considerations. This trend, common to all sectors of society, is particularly disquieting in a country where 35 million people are under-nourished, and where one million children a year are born to families who are underfed.[14]

Two factors are noted in the shift in the Mexican diet. First, there is the penetration of 130 transnational corporations (99 of them U.S. based), who have entered the Mexican market by setting up subsidiaries, taking over Mexican companies, or starting joint ventures with Mexican capital.

The second element in the new pattern of nutrition, are the millions of dollars spent on advertising by these corporations to promote their processed and packaged foods. Between 1970 and 1975, for example, consumption of popcorn, potato chips, and other processed foods increased by almost 27 percent. Yet researchers point out that a package of corn chips costs twenty times more than a kilo of more nutritious corn tortillas.[15]

As this account indicates, once the penetration of transnational capital occurs, it relies heavily on advertising expenditures in the mass media, to persuade local publics of the superiority of the new goods and services offered by the TNCs, as well as the life-styles associated with them (e.g., "The Pepsi Generation"). Inevitably and ineluctably, whatever the social need to the contrary, the resources and the energies of the exposed national community are redirected according to the dynamics and imperatives of the transnational corporate system. These are, first, foremost, and exclusively, the search for markets and profits.

This is not an overdrawn appraisal. Consider the following part of a dialogue between a reporter of the *New York Times* and the two chief executives of the Coca-Cola Company, one of the most well-known consumer good transnationals:

Question: Are changing demographics working against you and other soft drink companies?

Mr. Keough (President and Chief Operating Officer): We really look at demographics on a worldwide basis. Only 5 percent of the world's population is in the United States. As our business grows, it is inevitable that it is going to grow at a much faster rate abroad. Around the world, there are hugh chunks of population where the demographics are highly favorable. You take the whole continent of Africa and the Pacific Basin from Korea to Austrolasia. In Latin America, where we have a dominant position, the demographics for any consumer product that can be afforded by people there are highly favorable. In Brazil, the median age is under 18.[16]

And Coca-Cola, along with a few hundred other consumer goods transnationals, has the resources to saturate these "attractive" markets with the sales message for its products.

In sum, North American transnational capital, the new information technology, and national mass media systems dependent on TNC advertising financing, are the pillars—along with the never absent armed forces—of the prevailing international economic and information order.

THE NEED FOR FREE FLOW NOW MELDS THE
INDUSTRIAL, MEDIA, AND ADVERTISING SECTORS
OF AMERICAN CAPITALISM

The powerful transnational corporate system, its marketing apparatus, and the military presence around the globe that protects it, are now each dependent almost totally on massive, instantaneous, and international information flows. For this compelling reason, the "free flow of information" has become a doctrine essential to the maintenance of the powerful transnational system, constructed largely since World War II. Today, therefore, the free flow doctrine has been elevated to the highest level of U.S. foreign policy.

The free flow idea is no new construct. For half a century it has been a doctrine stoutly defended on behalf of the international marketing objectives of general media interests, though always presented as an issue of human rights and individual freedom. News agencies, film, and later TV producers, publishers, and record companies joined regularly in campaigns in the early post-war period to break down barriers to the export of their products. "Free flow" was the rhetorical instrument, alongside the economic clout of U.S. media conglomerates, to pry open closed European and formerly European-dominated ex-colonial markets.

Now, nothing less than the core interests of the American transnational corporate order are concerned with, because they are dependent on, a "free flow" for their business, marketing, and military information. A former Assistant Secretary of State for Economic Affairs told an Organization for Economic Cooperation and Development (OECD) meeting in 1980:

> First, the free flow of information is essential to the political, economic, and social health of all countries. This is a positive good...

> Second, so indispensable is the principle of free flow that it should enjoy a strong, positive bias in the international discussion.[17]

This view, unfailingly expressed at the highest governmental level for four decades, can be accepted as the cardinal principle of the U.S. national communications policy. Not unexpectedly, it is fully congruent with the needs of the most powerful American transnationals. Also in 1980, an IBM executive made this complementary statement to a Congressional Committee:

> My testimony will address these questions from the perspective of a corporation dependent upon international information flow. IBM does business in over 120 countries. We are, therefore, very dependent on a free flow of infor-

mation in order to maintain our operations worldwide. We need this flow of information in order to communicate worldwide engineering, design and manufacturing information as well as to inform our customers about technical changes and improvements to our products on which, in turn their operations depend. It is also necessary for us to match engineering, technological and marketing support skills with user requirements...We must have the ability to move financial and operational information among our various organizations as freely as possible. Finally, we must interact continuously with international banking and transportation facilities, such as airlines, which, in turn, also depend on a free flow of information to conduct their operations.[18]

To satisfy one of the more specialized, though hardly trivial, needs of the transnational corporate system, the free flow doctrine is amended and interpreted, on some occasions to include the "free flow of advertising." This is the view, at least, of Leonard S. Matthews, president of the American Association of Advertising Agencies, Inc. He writes about "the threat to a free flow of information—including commercial information..."[19]

The World Press Freedom Committee, too, its membership drawn from some of the largest and most influential North American media combines, is hardly reticent on this point.

Meeting in Talloires, France, in May 1981, with other Western media interests, the group declared: "We believe that the free flow of information is essential for mutual understanding and world peace." However, "free flow" cannot exist, according to these media owners and editors, without a "free press." And a free press, still according to the wisdom of this group, depends on the financial support of advertising. "We acknowledge," the Talloires Declaration states, "the importance of advertising as a consumer service and in providing financial support for a strong and self-sustaining press. Without financial independence, the press cannot be independent."[20]

In this reasoning, a free press requires advertising to sustain itself. Internationally as well as domestically, advertising is supplied, for the most part, by transnational corporations. And, since the TNC is the chief support of a free press, those individuals or nations, who fail to recognize the legitimacy and desirability of this linkage, have excluded themselves from the circle of freedom—defined, obligingly enough, by organizations such as the World Press Freedom Committee.

It is a persuasive construct. Transnational media corporations achieve their own profit-making ends while serving the message creation and transmission needs of the transnational system overall—the global private corporations in banking, transport, information, agri-business, energy, and consumer goods. These latter cannot function without advertising. It follows that advertising becomes defined, by the transnational system, as an indispensable component of "freedom." The media combines insist that advertising constitutes a pillar of press freedom.

Support for a transnational corporate definition of the free flow of information comes from the highest political level of the U.S. Government, the White House itself. In a letter addressed to the Speaker of the House of Representatives, the Honorable Thomas P. O'Neill, Jr., in September 1981, President Reagan wrote:

The United States has long regarded the principle of the free flow of information as a cornerstone of any democratic political order, and an essential instrument for further understanding among the peoples of the world and encouraging the growth of free, equitable and enlightened government... We strongly support—and commend the attention of all nations—the declaration issued by the independent media leaders of twenty-one nations at the Voices of Freedom Conference, which met at Talloires, France, in May of this year.[21]

The systemic concern for the protection of the free flow doctrine is not misplaced. Philip H. Power, newspaper owner and publisher, and sometimes member of the U.S. delegation to UNESCO, describes why:

The stakes in the coming battle go far beyond editors and publishers, who, so far, have been the only ones directly involved. They extend to the great computer and information hardware companies whose foreign sales of billions of dollars are at stake; to the TV networks and movie makers whose entertainment products range the globe; to the airlines and banks and financial institutions whose need for computer-to-computer data literally defines their business; to the multi-million-dollar international advertising industry.[22]

These considerations led Anthony Smith, director of the British Film Institute, to make this appraisal:

Oddly enough, the field of informatics, which represents the developed world at its most inexorably powerful, is also one in which the same countries are very vulnerable. For if the transformation of Western industrial economies or information economies is to succeed, they must eventually enjoy the benefits of a free flow of data.[23]

Hugh Donaghue of Control Data Corporation says much the same thing: "The basis for new management is a growing dependency on the free flow of information, and consequently, a growing vulnerability if this free flow is restricted or stopped completely."[24]

This, then, is the dilemma!

Strength comes from the great flexibility and control that the new information technologies provide to the worldwide business system. Vulnerability, however, accompanies this strength because there is also an enormous dependency of the system on unrestricted, open circuits for the flood of messages the system initiates and transmits. Vulnerability also resides in the necessity for *national* agreement for the transmission of messages as well as on the physical location of communication facilities, i.e., the stationing of satellites in specific spatial orbits.

For these reasons, international negotiations over information-communications issues touch the exposed nerves of the transnational corporate order.

A WORLD OF OBSTRUCTIONISTS

But why would the free flow be restricted, and who would intervene to do it? In the briefest terms, the miscreants are all those who object to the benefits and privileges that "free flow" confers on U.S. transnational enterprises and to the disadvantages and costs that are perceived to accrue to those nations and classes affected by transnational corporate activity. The obstructionists—and potential obstructionists—are a surprisingly diverse group. For Americans, accustomed as they are to casting communists as the primary instigators of global, national, and community trouble, this anti-free-flow coalition presents a disconcerting pluralism.

An example of those who are outspoken in their concern over the flow of information across national borders is Jan Freese, director-general of the Swedish Data Inspection Board and formerly a judge. He has often said that "it seems to be a paradox, but nevertheless the free flow of information ...has to be regulated by international agreements in order to be kept free."[25]

Our close Canadian neighbors, with whom we share a 3000-mile open border, also have forceful views on "free flow." Although Canadians are naturally far from unanimous, official statements indicate a wide divergence from the U.S. position. An extraordinary committee was created by the Canadian minister of communications in 1978 to study the implications of telecommunications for Canadian sovereignty. Known as the Clyne Committee, it reported this in 1979: "Telecommunications, as the foundation of the future society, cannot always be left to the vagaries of the market; principles that we might care to assert in other fields, such as totally free competition, may not be applicable in this crucial sphere."

The committee was especially concerned with transborder data flow, dataprocessing services, and external control of national information data banks. "Few people in Canada," it states, "are aware of the implications of what is happening." The committee urged that "protective measures" be taken. The committee concluded its report with some powerful language seldom seen in a government document:

We see communication as one of the fundamental elements of sovereignty, and we are speaking of the sovereignty of the people of a country...We urge the Government of Canada to take immediate action to alert the people of Canada to the perilous position of their collective sovereignty that has resulted from the new technologies of telecommunications and informatics.[26]

The French have been no less critical and apprehensive of the workings of the free-flow doctrine. A paper on transborder data flow written in 1980 by Alain Madec, a senior French official, received this comment in a U.S. congressional study:

From the perspective of those concerned with the free flow of information and the liberalization of trade, the tone of the draft is disturbing. While asserting a deep regard for the principle of the free flow of information, the report deftly suggests that the world needs to move away from that principle, stating that: "...other complimentary [sic] values cannot be ignored, i.e., the responsibility of sovereign states, the balance of advantage to be derived from mutually profitable trade, and respect for the diversity of peoples and cultures.[27]

This is but one of the innumerable official French comments in recent years which have questioned the free-flow doctrine.

Canadian, Swedish, and French leaders have indicated their concern over U.S. domination in the economic and information fields. As might be expected, Third World leaders from Latin America, Asia, and Africa express even more critical views. They have reason to do so. Their societies are not competitive with the transnational system in any respect. With few exceptions, they experience the full weight and costs of the transnational companies in their midst.

There are, to be sure, important differences in the views of the hundred-plus bloc of national states on free flow, as there are on most other political, economic, and cultural questions. In more than a dozen high-level international meetings of nonaligned and Third World leaders, the free flow of information as it occurs today has been identified as a mechanism for informational penetration, cultural domination, and economic exploitation.[28] This criticism, which began in Algiers in 1973, was reiterated at Yaounde, Cameroon, in July 1980. "The grip of the multinationals on world communication" was cited there as a major obstacle to global informational equality. The conferees urged "a radical change in the relationship of communication to knowledge, money, and power."[29]

FREE FLOW'S EMBATTLED FRONTS

Whether a "radical change in the relationship of communication to knowledge, money, and power" is imminent, is an open question. What is beyond debate are the increasingly frequent international interventions that challenge the assumptions and institutionalized operating arrangements underpinning the transnational corporate free flow of information. These interventions can be grouped around content, structural, and regulatory issues.

For a long time the *content* of international communication flows has been excluded as a legitimate subject for discussion and international consideration. The Western interpretation of individual freedom of speech prevailed. Yet the fact that the overwhelming bulk of international information flows are *not* individual but corporate, makes the Western defense of free flow less persuasive.

It is in this context that support developed for setting standards for the *quality* of the information flowing between nations. On November 22, 1978, after almost a decade of debate and innumerable textual revisions, at the twentieth session of the General Conference of UNESCO, in Paris, the *Declaration on Fundamental Principles Concerning The Contribution of the Mass Media to Strengthening Peace and International Understanding, to the Promotion of Human Rights and to Countering Racialism, Apartheid and Incitement to War,* was adopted by acclamation.[30]

This is not the place for an extended analysis of the Declaration nor of the compromises that had to be made by all signatories for it to be adopted. It is sufficient to note that despite many ambiguities and even contradictions in the text of the Declaration, one precedent-making perspective was agreed to in the draft. This is the acceptance of the view that the *content* of the mass media and by extension, of international information flows in general, are ultimately accountable to an international humanistic standard.

Corporate and commercial message-making and information flows can now, at least in principle, be separated from the deservedly privileged status of *individual* free expression, and subjected to scrutiny and, if necessary, rejection. When and how this will develop are still unclear. Yet the principle has been established in an international document.

To be sure, this principle has not been accepted with unbounded enthusiasm in the Western market economies. In fact, in the United States, it has reinforced the existing suspicion and opposition to international decision-making that now colors a great part of the official outlook.

Yet it appears more and more likely, that the content of international communication increasingly, will be an area of national oversight and autonomous decision-making. The "infant baby formula" controversy is another pointer in this direction.

In this widely debated case, the issue was one of international advertising of a product, prepared infant's formula, that could have serious health consequences when used because of inadequate infrastructural conditions—i.e., potable water—in many of the countries in which the product was being promoted.

After years of debate, the World Health Organization (WHO) drafted a code, open for national adoption. In it, the sale of infant formula was not forbidden, but aggressive forms of marketing and advertising the product were restricted. When the issue came to a vote in the WHO in May of 1981, the U.S. voted *alone* against the code—118 to 1. The United States delegate explained his negative vote this way: The "central basis" for Washington's opposition was the serious concerns felt over WHO's "involvement in commercial codes."[31]

From a TNC perspective, the concern was well-founded. The infant formula industry in that year was a $1.4 billion worldwide market.[32] Yet much more than this was and is at stake.

Calling international advertising to account, even in so flagrant a case as "baby formula" marketing, signals danger to the entire global marketing system. It is an early warning sign that the issue of Western information control is taking on a new dimension.

For several years, that control has been protested in international forums and organizations. But until the infant formula issue and the mass media declaration, the complaints have consisted mainly of questioning the preponderance of Western media products in world markets, exclusive Western versions of the news, and the largely one-way flow of messages from a few industrialized centers to the rest of the world.

Efforts to create a new international information order in the past have emphasized the provision of additional sources of programming for news and entertainment, support of local and national cultural institutions, and the utilization of improved communication technologies.[33]

What has been missing from this generally constructive work, has been a recognition of the interrelatedness of the world economy and the motor force of its dynamic, supplied by the transnational corporate system. With the inclusion of message content as a basis for national oversight of information flow, the struggle for a new international information order merges with the search for a new international economic order. When these demands are joined, nothing less than the transnational corporate system itself, becomes the focus of challenge and contestation.

If the infant formula code initiative is a foretaste of what may face the international advertising industry, the still more vital sphere of corporate transborder data flows—all the messages passing across national frontiers, mostly by electronic means—is likely to prove an equally provocative issue. In these flows, which affect production, finance, investment, and industrial policy, nothing less than national autonomy is involved.

For example, the sanctions imposed in 1982, by the U.S. government on European nations continuing to uphold their contracts for supplying equipment for the Euro-Siberian gas pipeline, revealed how the control of information flows, in a computerized transnational system, may operate to the disadvantage of the dependent party.

The government merely instructed the parent firm in the United States, to turn off the information supply to its affiliate. *Business Week* reported the action this way:

> All Dresser (Dresser Industries, Inc.) had to do to comply with Reagan's embargo was to change the entry key to a computer in Pittsburgh on August 26 (1982), the day the sanctions took effect. That effectively barred Dresser's French subsidiary from access to the technology it needs to complete orders it has on the books and to compete for new ones...Without access to Dresser's computerized data bank, Dresser-France's engineers lack vital information to build the made-to-order compressors that account for about three-quarters of the company's business.[34]

If this can happen to a "core" country in Western Europe, what may be the fate of the hundred or more less industrialized countries in which the advanced informational systems and connections with the metropole centers are now being installed?

A Brazilian study on transnational data flows touches directly on this:

> transborder data flow links are not only used to move data internationally, but also to shift such information resources as managerial and engineering skills; computer power, technology developments, data-base management systems, specialized software and intelligence in general. Given the prevailing global distribution and administration of information and skills, transborder data flows tend to facilitate their concentration in developed countries...If projected linearly, this could lead, in the long run, to an intellectual impoverishment of the societies of developing countries.[35]

Can information flows of such vital interest to national decision-making and national class interests be expected to remain unchecked and unmolested far into the future? All signs point in the other direction. And as the global market competition intensifies, national efforts to intervene may be expected to accelerate. As early as 1978, a Canadian Consultative Committee on the Implications of Telecommunications for Canadian sovereignty recommended that "the Government should act immediately to regulate transborder data flows to ensure that we do not lose control of information vital to the maintenance of national sovereignty."[36]

No drastic implementation of this recommendation has yet occurred. Elsewhere too, the opposition to unrestricted transborder data flows remains largely rhetorical, but this should not be taken to mean that the issue will remain basically quiescent. Too much is at stake, and many other information flow developments are converging that make the issue paramount.

INTERNATIONAL INFORMATION FLOW
INFRASTRUCTURE

Direct broadcasting from communication satellites in space, for example, is now a realizable technology, expected to be in operation in the years immediately ahead. Yet direct satellite broadcasting opens national territory to the signals of external message-makers who have the financial resources and technological capability of transmitting images and programming directly into individual homes, circumventing national authority and supervision.

Not surprisingly, the sentiment in the international community outside the U.S. is practically unanimous in a preference for what is called "prior consent"—the right of the receiving society, and its national representatives, to decide *in advance* whether to accept the direct broadcast signal.

On the subjecct of direct broadcasting from satellites, the United States is almost alone in its insistence that there should be no rule of "prior consent" and that to allow such an international stipulation would be a serious infringement of the free flow of information and even a violation of the U.S. Constitution's protection of the right of free speech, i.e., the First Amendment.

The applicability of the U.S. Constitution to the world-at-large, without the world having a say in the matter, is in itself, indicative of the distance that separates U.S. policy from world realities. A non-binding declaration of "principles governing the use by States of artificial earth satellites for international direct television broadcasting" was adopted by the United Nations General Assembly in December 1982. One hundred and eight (108) nations endorsed the right of nations to *prior consent* over incoming, direct broadcast satellite messages. The United States and a small number of supporting nations were in the minority.[37]

Actually, the introduction of direct satellite broadcasting on a global scale depends on many technical, economic, and political factors that still have to be taken into account. All that can be said at this time is that the capability of DBS presents still another immeasurable challenge to national sovereignty, that is not likely to be ignored.

Consider for example, the production mounted in early 1982 by the U.S. government, to utilize the Polish martial law crisis to further exacerbate Soviet-Western relations. The overtly provocative hour and a half TV program, "Let Poland Be Poland" was beamed by satellite to more than 50 countries—the costs of transmission being borne by the U.S. government. Yet it remained a national decision in Europe and elsewhere, whether the transmission of the program to local audiences would be allowed. With direct broadcasting from satellites, and no agreement on prior consent, the decision would have been completely in the hands of the U.S. government (or, hypothetically, even a private initiative).

There are other infrastructural issues in international communication, affecting information flows, which illuminate the fragility of the existing arrangements and the strong likelihood of future instability and crisis. There is, for example, the question of the allocation of orbital slots for the increasing number of communication satellites being thrust into the sky. The already great and continuously expanding volume of international electronic flows of information, depend on submarine cable and communication satellites—increasingly the latter. Yet the number of prime positions available for the location of satellites in geostationary orbit, is not unlimited. At present, "first come, first served" is the rule and de facto operating principle. Not unexpectedly, it is strongly espoused by the United States, which has the technological capability to be "first." While this approach is most agreeable to the Pentagon and the TNCs, a broad front of international sentiment, in the less industrialized as well as the more industrially advanced countries, is much less enthusiastic.

Closely related to the "orbital slot" allocation issue, is how nations, once they have access to satellites, will share the various radio, television, and microwave frequencies that allow information to be beamed to and from the satellites. On frequency use, national needs differ as do the requirements of special user groups *within* the nation. About these questions, there are shifting national and individual group interests. On specific issues, unexpected coalitions of ordinarily adversary participants may be formed.

All the same, the current privileged position of the United States and a few other advanced industrial nations, is being contested with increasing intensity. International conferences involving telecommunications, in earlier times, were meetings in which a few powerful states, generally in a relaxed setting, agreed, or sometimes disagreed, among themselves, on how to manage world communications. Always it was asserted that the deliberations were technical, could be made only by engineers, and politics were unnecessary and diversionary. As the few industrially developed nations obtained everything they wanted, they described the arrangements as efficient and nonpolitical.

All this has begun to change. In the 1970s, culminating in the World Administrative Radio Conference (WARC) in 1979, the voices of the hitherto excluded began to be heard, if not seriously listened to. At this time, it was discovered by the U.S. and a few Western European states, that the discussions had become "politicized," that is, demands were being made to make the decisions more even-handed and more equitable to the 135 or so, less privileged member states.

AMERICAN RESPONSES TO THE GROWING OPPOSITION TO THE RULES AND ARRANGEMENTS THAT ENABLE TRANSNATIONAL CORPORATE INFORMATION DOMINATION

By the end of the 1970s, it was apparent (to anyone allowing for such an eventuality) that there was almost universal opposition to the prevailing international information structure and to the principle of free flow that undergirds it. Though some in the U.S. at that time, persisted in regarding this opposition as "paranoic," "obsessive," and reflecting a preoccupation with a "bogeyman" issue,[38] others began to develop a more realistic assessment.

A December 1980 report of the Committee on Government Operations of the U.S. House of Representatives noted the following:

> Whatever the particular perspective of a country, an increasing number of nations worry that the loss of control over information about internal functions can jeopardize their sovereignty and leave them open to possible disruptions, ranging from uncontrollable technical failures to political sabotage.

The Committee recognized that privacy protection, national sovereignty, external control of domestic activities, national security, technology transfer, and "cultural erosion...are common concerns not limited to the Third World."[39]

Another indication of changing sentiment came from Anthony G. Oettinger, chairman of Harvard University's Program on Information Resources Policy, who wrote:

> The resulting conflict between the principles of free flow of information and of national sovereignty is fueled by the fear, expressed by many states, that the United States would use its great technological advantage in this area for political, cultural, or commercial purposes...Consequently, the restrictionist impulses of most of the world [are pitted] against an increasingly isolated American devotion to a principle of free flow of information.[40]

Morris H. Crawford's view represented another step forward in awareness at that time. Crawford was formerly executive secretary of the U.S. Department of State's Interagency Task Force and Public Advisory Group on International Information Flow, and is now a consultant on information technology trade. He acknowledged that "a reweighing past applications of the free flow doctrine is long overdue," and went on to say:

> The doctrine itself arises from constitutional principles that no sensible person seriously questions. But these principles have to be applied realistically in terms of the actual channels through which information flows. Other govern-

ments, while continuing to respect our constitutional principles, have shown with startling unanimity and unmistakable clarity that they want to take a fresh look at modern application of these principles. Our isolation has grown in the two years since U.N. debates on direct broadcasting via satellites found the U.S. deserted even by its staunchest allies...U.S. assumptions about free flow need to be reassessed in the context of modern communication technologies and their impact on other members of the interdependent world community. The U.S. is out of phase in an international reexamination in which we have more at stake than any other country. Paradoxically, failure to face the reality of changing definitions of free flow tends to strengthen the hands of those who favor stronger controls over all forms of global information exchange.[41]

But, if the free flow of information is a vital support to the global overlordship of American transnational companies, how much room is there for adjustment?

Crawford is among those policymakers and other influential people in the United States who think there is space to maneuver. He urges "a comprehensive theme and unifying purpose" for U.S. policy. We should define the boundaries within which some "international rules for communication and information flows might be acceptable." There should also be "coordination and monitoring of U.S. planning and negotiating activities that affect international communication."[42]

Robert Manning, former editor of the *Atlantic Monthly,* and associated with State Department thinking over a long time, also has taken up the question of the concessions that may have to be made to keep the overall system intact. He writes:

There is still time, it appears, for Western government and communications giants to cure this intolerable imbalance by constructing the new communication networks "in a spirit of real interdependence and bringing the people of the Third World into the manufacture, installation and some of the operations of the new electronic technology."[43]

Manning understood that this could involve "some uncomfortable concessions" on such matters as the distribution of radio frequencies and partnerships with Third World governments. "Stockholders might not care for such arrangements," he added, "but their managements plainly should be thinking about forestalling the conflicts and calamities that [may be in the offing]."

These perspectives, reviewed now, toward the end of the first Reagan administration, can be regarded as an expression of sweet reasonableness in U.S. official and semi-official thinking and action, that lasted a very short time indeed. Coincidentally, with the thinking outlined above, was another outlook expressing a hardening approach to those criticizing existing information structures and arrangements.

It was evident, for example, at the conclusion of the World Administrative Radio Conference in 1979. At that time, the United States government reevaluated its relationship to the International Telecommunications Union (ITU), the organization with responsibility for the allocation and management of the international radio frequency spectrum and the geostationary orbit for communication satellites.

An official study, prepared by the Office of Technology Assessment for the United States Senate Committee on Commerce, Science, and Transportation, came to these conclusions: The world has changed. There are scores of new, independent, poor nations participating in international regulatory and administrative organizations. They seek to change the existing allocation of benefits and privileges, which are lopsidedly in favor of a few, industrialized states and the most powerful users in those countries. The United States is not only unwilling to make these concessions but, in fact, seeks to obtain a greater share of scarce global resources to meet the needs of its transnational enterprises and its global military force. And, finally, in international gatherings where these issues are discussed, and (at least in the past) decided upon, the likelihood of United States' interests getting their way, grows more doubtful.[44]

The no-nonsense, straightforward comments of the study are worth quoting in detail:

> The world environment for telecommunications has changed significantly in recent years; two-thirds of the 155 member nations of ITU can be classified as developing or Third World countries. There were 65 nations and seven groups of colonies present at the 1947 Atlantic City Conference, 80 nations and five groups of colonies at the 1959 WARC, and 142 nations (no colonies) at WARC-79.

> There are basic differences between the United States and Third World countries over the principles that should govern the allocation and use of the radio spectrum and related satellite orbit capacity.

> Third World Countries are increasingly able to influence and shape international communication policies in international forums.

> The United States must maintain its technological leadership and expand its influence if future actions in a "one-nation-one-vote" forum like ITU are to be favorable to U.S. positions.

> There has been a gradual shift toward recognizing the legitimacy of nontechnical factors such as political and cultural interests and values in ITU deliberations and other international forums.

U.S. requirements for access to the frequency spectrum and geostationary satellite orbit locations are expanding with the explosive growth in telecommunications/information technology, the growing use of satellites, and the increasing dependence on radio and satellites for military and national security purposes.

The disparity between nations in their ability to use the spectrum is growing: this leads to growing disagreement over the allocation and use of specific frequency bands for specific services.

Spectrum decisions arrived at as a result of voting within the ITU, as opposed to the commonly practiced consensus approach, will tend to be increasingly adverse to the US.

What to do?
The Assessment Panel outlined a few options:

- Abandon the ITU altogether "and establish a more congenial grouping of developed countries as a forum for coordination to avoid radio interference, and simply ignore other countries."
- Abandon the "one-nation, one-vote" formula, and change the voting system "to one more fair to the United States perhaps giving added voting weight to those countries that contribute most heavily to the United Nations budget."
- Force a revision of the "one-nation, one-vote" formula to one that would reflect the dominance of these nations in the actual use of the spectrum.[45]

In sum, the recommendations proposed by the assessment panel, for U.S. adoption in the ITU, advocate anti-democratic voting procedures, and, failing their adoption, the abandonment of international agreement in favor of unilateral decisions based on economic and technological strength.

Attacks, governmental and private, on international organizations responsible for information and information-related matters, multiply inside the United States. The ITU, UNESCO, and the United Nations itself—to the extent each takes positions responsive to its own majority constituency, come under bitter criticism in the U.S.

Indicative of official American governmental sentiment to the UN's handling of information matters, was a vote at the end of December 1981 on a draft resolution on *Questions Relating to Information*. The resolution contained, among many matters concerned with the world information situation, an increased budget for the UN Committee on Information—to enable it to cope with the continuously growing number of information issues. The vote showed 147 nations in favor of the resolution and two against (Israel and the United States). There were no abstentions.[46]

In this instance, as reported in the *Chronicle of International Communication,* itself an organ which reflects establishment thinking on international communication issues, American "officials emphasize that these [the recommendations in the Resolution] draw heavily on language and resolutions adopted at the UN in previous years, when, in their thinking, U.S. negotiators acceded to an aggregation of semantic nuances and ideological fine points that now foster Third World control of UN information resources while eroding global press freedom."[47]

Less elegantly phrased, (Reagan) officials in the 1980s are repudiating resolutions and principles agreed to by United States representatives in earlier meetings and discussions at the UN.

In the same vein, transnational corporations have grown more outspoken and now advance their (informational) interests publicly. A five-page advertisement, in color, in *Time* magazine (February 1, 1982), paid for by the Smith-Kline corporation, a medical supplies and pharmaceutical transnational, promoted the communication declaration of the World Press Freedom Committee, the so-called Talloires Declaration. The spread spotlighted what it termed "Danger at the UN," and contributed its bit to the furtherance of public mistrust and suspicion of international organization and agreement.

The United States first threatened to withdraw the American financial contribution to UNESCO in 1981, if that organization persisted in questioning the absolute desirability of the U.S. media combines' free flow doctrine.[48]

The threat became an actuality at the end of 1983. For weeks earlier, the public was prepared for the announcement by articles questioning UNESCO's utility, judiciously inserted in the "quality" newspapers and over the airwaves. The *New York Times* was properly "balanced" in its editorial support for the abandonment of UNESCO:

> A United States withdrawal would not harm any democratic cause or global understanding. If fairly explained, it might even promote scientific and cultural values.[49]

The U.S. assault on international bodies engaged in information issues, is accompanied by a forceful unilateralist position—expressed sometimes as a preference for bilateral negotiation—one on one—often, as a go-it-alone, take it or leave it proposition.

The latter predilection, by no means limited to information issues, is presented boldly in this sphere, especially with respect to the "free flow of information" doctrine. Here, the inclination to regard the domestic legal arrangements which support free flow, as inviolable codes, applicable intact, to the international scene, grows increasingly audacious.

This takes the form of insisting on the international applicability and desirability of the U.S. Constitution's First Amendment—the free speech clause—interpreted by the transnational corporations as freedom for commercial speech.

Views such as this, and the actions based on them, led a Royal Institute of International Affairs study to conclude that the United States has adopted an "assertive" extraterritorial jurisdiction, which has increased over the last 40 years and "the trend has clearly been upward."[50]

"Extraterritoriality" is defined as "...the general problem of conflicting claims by nation-states to apply their laws and implement their policies to affect conduct outside their territory in a way which may undermine and conflict with the laws and policies of a foreign government" (p. viii).

Extraterritoriality is no new feature of international relations. Now, a new context prevails but the claims are familiar. The United States' "aggressive approach to extraterritorial enforcement" (p. 8) is a function of the power of the American transnational system. It arises because "...the wealthier and more powerful you are, the more difficult it is for others to resist your actions." Accordingly, "U.S. extraterritoriality increased as the United States became an international power; and as European nations were especially dependent upon the United States for economic assistance— during the 1940s and early 1950s" (p. 9).

Yet the ability to maintain and extend United States' information-communications domination by resorting to the extraterritorial invocation of U.S. law is no longterm guarantee for maintaining present privileges in the international economic and informational order.

For law, no less than communication, can become a two-way street. "Those countries which see themselves as victims of extraterritoriality," write the authors of the study on that subject, "are becoming more vigorous in their responses" (p. 31).

Indeed, how far can unilateralism in the promotion of international information flows be pushed? Ultimately, it is confronted with an unresolvable contradiction. The United States transnational corporate system cannot maintain itself in a fervent unilateralist environment. The system requires internationalism—its own brand of internationalism, to be sure. The concept of "interdependence" was created to describe favorably, as well as to conceal, the relationships imposed by international capital on its dependencies.

United States-owned transnational capital needs international communications. If it acts to disrupt international cooperation in information flows too forcefully, it is striking at its own existence. As Dallas Smythe asks, "...could it be, to plagiarize Mao Zedong, that monopoly capitalism has become, not a paper tiger, but an electronic information tiger?"[51]

Still, it would be unrealistic to imagine that the restraints generated by the system's application of power foretell an imminent crisis and an early demise of the transnational order. It still possesses enormous material and ideological power.

Many stratagems remain available to the managers of the transnational corporate system to contain and limit the growing opposition to the free flow doctrine.

One step in this direction, is the effort to separate the free flow doctrine's application to the media industries on the one hand, and the users of commercial information—transborder data flows, for the most part—on the other. The first category is seen as ideological and inviolable. The second as pragmatic and negotiable. Oswald Ganley, formerly an Assistant Secretary of State, makes this nuanced differentiation:

> As time passes, there is a growing dichotomy between two sets of interests within the United States vis-a-vis activities in international bodies. This is taking place in the free flow of information.
>
> The print and electronic media, and those engaged in news gathering and advertising, cite the First Amendment. They say that access to information is a basic right of all people, and quote Article 19 of the Universal Declaration of Human Rights. . . .
>
> They see free flow in ideological terms and feel that if you tamper in the slightest with these rights, then the whole card house of freedom will come tumbling down.
>
> On the other hand, those primarily interested in the free flow of commercial information seek free flow, but they do from a very different mind set. They look at this as a pragmatic rather than an ideological matter. They say it is not really a First Amendment problem—although they will use the First Amendment when it seems appropriate! They say that free flow is essential to modern commerce in the same sense as open sea lanes and open skies, and that modern commerce and the running of the world's multinational corporations demand this openness. Therefore, they say, ways must be found and the appropriate compromises made with other countries to keep open such free information flow.[52]

How strong is the transnational corporate willingness to compromise and how far it might go are still to be discovered. Whatever, it seems unlikely that it can overcome, or even significantly reduce, the opposition to free flow that already exists and that is bound to grow. Yet, how rapidly further resistance to free flow will develop and whether it can force fundamental changes in the existing international information system, are also unknown at this time.

NOTES TO CHAPTER FOUR

1. William C. Salmon, "International Aspects of Communications and Information," working paper, Washington, D.C., February 24, 1983, p. 3.

2. Mark Fowler, before the Subcommittee on Government Information and Individual Rights, House of Representatives, September 22, 1981.

3. Suggestive of this observation, is the announcement of the appointment of a new chairman of the Foreign Policy Association (FPA). The FPA is one of the oldest and most distinguished "think tanks" of the American foreign policy establishment. It has generally been assigned the responsibility of identifying significant emerging problems, areas and issues that could unsettle the U.S. corporate presence abroad and America's international position in general. In February 1982, the Association chose Leonard Marks as its new chairman. Marks, a former director of the United States Information Agency, more recently an executive of the American media combine's World Press Freedom Association, has been associated closely with corporate and governmental media interests and policymaking for thirty years. Media and foreign policy are now joined, symbolically at least, in his appointment to FPA's highest position.

4. W. Michael Blumenthal, "Transborder Data Flows and the New Protectionism," *Vital Speeches of the Day,* Speech delivered before the National Computer Conference, Chicago, Illinois, May 6, 1981.

5. Klaus Sahlgren, "Role of UNCTC in TDF," *TDR,* Vol. 7, No. 7, October/November, 1982, p. 350.

6. "Why American Express Depends on Telecommunications," *TDR* Report, Vol. 6, No. 1, January/February, 1983, p. 18.

7. "U.S. Reluctant over TDF Study," quoting *Computerworld,* September 27, 1982, *TDR,* October/November, 1982, Vol. 5, No. 7, p. 323; and "Volume of Corporate TDF Dropped from OECD Survey," *TDR,* Vol. 5, No. 5, July/August, 1982, p. 220.

8. Marc Burbridge, "Roundup In Rio," *Datamation,* March, 1983, pp. 189–198.

9. "*International Data Flow,*" Statement of Robert E. L. Walker, Hearings before a subcommittee of the Committee on Government Operations, House of Representatives, Ninety-Sixth Congress, 2nd Session, March-April, 1980, pp. 112–113.

10. The *New York Times,* March 13, 1983. The present magnitude and expected growth of the information sector is indicated in these figures: "The world market for telecommunications and computer products and services, now worth almost $380 billion, is expected to reach $650 billion by 1987. In 1980, advanced-technology [U.S.] manufacturers showed a positive Balance of Trade of $31 billion, while in the same year, all other manufactured goods showed a deficit of $50 billion. Computers and Office machinery alone, showed a positive Balance of Trade of over $6 billion in 1981."
Oswald H. Ganley, "Political Resolution of Communications and Information Disputes," *TDR,* Vol. 6, No. 6, September, 1983, p. 347.

11. Harry L. Freeman, "GATT Rule on Service Is Crucial," *International Herald Tribune,* February 3, 1983.

12. Robert J. Coen, "Vast U.S. and Worldwide Ad Expenditures Expected," *Advertising Age,* November 13, 1980, pp. 10–16.

13. Joseph Fitchett, "Private Italian TV Firms Press for Freer Rein," The *International Herald Tribune,* March 15, 1982.

14. Mario de Cautin, "Mexico: High-Cost Processed Foods Replace Traditional Staples," *Interlink Press Service,* No. 9, December, 1981, pp. 10-13.

15. *Ibid.*

16. "Talking Business With Goizueta and Keough of Coca-Cola," The *New York Times,* December 1, 1981.

17. Matthew Nimetz, "International Communication Policy," October 6, 1980, United States Department of State, Bureau of Public Affairs, Washington, D.C., Policy No. 245.

18. John Rankine (Director of Standards, Product Safety and Data Security, IBM Corporation), *International Data Flow, op. cit.,* p. 32.

19. Leonard S. Matthews, "Designing a Muzzle for Media," *Business Week,* June 15, 1981, p. 18.

20. Text of Declaration by "Independent News Organizations on Freedom of the Press," The *New York Times,* May 18, 1981.

21. The White House, Washington, D.C., September 17, 1981.

22. Philip H. Power, "Threat To Ad Freedom?" *Advertising Age,* December 15, 1980.

23. Anthony Smith, *The Geopolitics Of Information,* New York, Oxford, 1980, p. 130.

24. Hugh P. Donaghue, "The Business Community's Stake in Global Communication," Paper delivered at the 43rd Annual Meeting, U.S. National Commission for UNESCO, Athens, Georgia, December 12, 1979, p. 5.

25. Jan Freese, "The Present and Future Swedish Data Policy," in *Data Regulation: European and Third World Realities,* Uxbridge, England, On-line, 1978, p. 81.

26. *"Telecommunications and Canada,"* Consultative Committee on the Implications of Telecommunications for Canadian Sovereignty (The Clyne Report), Ottawa, Canada, March, 1979, pp. 2, 63-64, 75-76.

27. *"International Information Flow: Forging A New Framework,"* Thirty-Second Report of the Committee on Government Operations, 96th Congress, 2nd Session, House Report No. 96-1535, December 11, 1980, Washington, D.C., U.S. Government Printing Office, p. 33.

28. Herbert I. Schiller, *"Decolonization of Information: Efforts Toward A New International Order,"* Latin American Perspectives, Vol. V, No. 1, Winter, 1978.

29. Intergovernmental Conference on Communication Policies in Africa, Yaounde, Cameroon, UNESCO, July 22-31, 1980.

30. *New Communication Order 9,* Historical Background of the Mass Media Declaration, Paris, UNESCO, 1982.

31. "U.S. Casts 'no' Vote as W.H.O. Approves Baby-Formula Code," The *New York Times,* May 21, 1981.

32. Robert Reinhold, "Furor Over Baby Formula—Where, When & How," The *New York Times*, May 24, 1981.

33. Sean McBride, *Many Voices, One World*, Paris, Kogan Page/Unipub-/ UNESCO, 1980, Amadou-Mahtar M'Bow, *Building the Future*, Paris, UNESCO, 1981.

34. "A Delivery That May Be Dresser-France's Last," *Business Week*, October 18, 1982, p. 50.

35. "Brazil: The Role of TNCs, TDF Impacts and Effects of National Policies," *Transnational Data Report*, Vol. 5, No. 7, October/November, 1982, pp. 329–335.

36. Canadian Department of Communications. Consultative Committee on Canadian Sovereignty, *Report on Telecommunications and Canada*, 1978.

37. Eric Pace, "UN General Assembly Endorses Curb on Satellite TV Broadcasts," *International Herald Tribune*, December 13, 1982.

38. Ithiel de Sola Pool, "Exporting Data—Latest Paranoia," *Telecommunication Policy*, Vol. 4, December, 1980, p. 314.

39. *International Information Flow: Forging A New Framework*, 32nd Report of the Committee on Government Operations, 96th Congress, 2nd Session, House Report No. 96-1535, December 11, 1980, pp. 19–23.

40. Anthony G. Oettinger, "Information Resources: Knowledge and Power in the 21st Century," *Science*, Vol. 209, July 4, 1980, p. 191–198.

41. Morris H. Crawford, "Toward an Information Age Debate," *Chronicle of International Communication*, Vol. 1, December 3, 1980, p. 2.

42. *Ibid.*

43. Robert Manning, "Data is Wealth and Power," Review of Anthony Smith's *The Geopolitics of Information*, in The *New York Times Book Review*, December 7, 1980, pp. 15, 38–39.

44. *Radiofrequency Use and Management: Impacts from the World Administrative Radio Conference of 1979, Summary*, Office of Technology Assessment, Congressional Board of the 97th Congress, Washington, D.C., Congress of the United States, 1980, pp. 8–9.

45. *Ibid*, pp. 18–19.

46. *Questions Relating To Information*, (A/36/819) December 12, 1981, Agenda Item 6, UN General Assembly, 36th Session.

47. Letter of the President of the United States to the Speaker of the House of Representatives, *op. cit.* Sept. 17, 1981.

48. Bernard Gwertzman, "U.S. In Quitting UNESCO, Affirms Backing for U.N.," The *New York Times*, December 30, 1983.

49. "Little Education, Science or Culture," The *New York Times*, December 16, 1983.

50. Douglas E. Rosenthal and William M. Knighton, *National Laws and International Commerce: The Problem of Exraterritoriality*, Chatham House Papers: 17, The Royal Institute of International Affairs, London, Routledge and Kegan Paul, 1982, p. 1.

51. Dallas Smythe, *Dependency Road: Communications, Capitalism, Conscious-ness, and Canada.* Norwood, New Jersey, Ablex, 1981, Appendix, p. 312.

52. Oswald Ganley, *op cit.,* p. 346.

Chapter Five

The Political Economy of Communication: Culture *Is* the Economy

In the Spring of 1983, French President Francois Mitterand told an international cultural symposium at the Sorbonne that, "The cultural industries are the industries of the future. Investing in culture is investing in the economy."[1]

A year earlier, Jack Lang, at the time French Minister of Culture, speaking of the efforts of dependent nations to liberate themselves, expressed the same idea, though in a context of conflict: "Economy and culture [are] the same struggle."[2]

This is not an exclusive national perspective, though for special reasons, it is more explicitly expressed in France than elsewhere. The fact is that capitalism, in its latest development, is transforming the process of cultural creation. At the same time, cultural production increasingly has become indistinguishable from industrial production and the cultural industries have become sites of great growth and high profitability.

This comes after a century or more of developments that could be considered preparatory for what is now occurring. Since the 19th century, higher productivity throughout the economy, the need and the financial ability of larger numbers of people to be consumers of culture, and the discovery of new means of reproduction of symbols, images, and sound have resulted in a vast increase in the production and consumption of cultural goods. Almost inevitably, the process of cultural creation increasingly adopted market methods and organizational structures characteristic of the productive mode of the rest of the capitalist economy.

However, in the last twenty years, there has been a critical new development. The nucleus of culture in a highly industrialized society—information itself—is being turned into a good of commerce, that is, an item for sale. With this new feature, new at least on the scale in which it is occurring, a qualitative change in every element of the process of cultural production follows.

Equally farreaching, the definition of what constitutes a cultural item, also is being transformed. The home television set, for example, increasingly becomes a display unit for computerized entertainment and informational outputs.

This chapter considers, in what can only be a tentative way, some of the new fundamental relationships and consequences of these changes.

Across the spectrum of industrial and cultural activities there is a progressive reduction of processes to a common dependence on the new information technologies *and* the market principles that now govern their use. Plant production, office work, professional service, home entertainment, and creative endeavor in the arts are characterized increasingly by their common utilization of, and dependence on, similar, if not identical equipment, systems, and processes. However, the most important commonality of all amongst these otherwise diverse sectors is in their reliance on, and specific utilization of, commercially-produced information.

Thus, the cultures of the home, the factory, the office, the school, and the street, in their utilization of electronics, as it is currently embodied in the new technologies, are, at the same time, adopting commercial modes and networks that integrate and "rationalize" human consciousness, no less than industrial production.

Moreover, this is occurring in a manner in which the impression is conveyed that an irresistible, extra-human, technological imperative is at work. A sheath of technological mystification obscures the rapid extension of capitalist criteria and control to terrain hitherto far less subject to its influence —the cultural process, and consciousness itself.

The speed with which this envelopment occurs is dictated by numerous forces, the most important of which at this time, probably is the pressure of chronic crisis felt throughout the world market system. This compels the individual firm, as well as the national economy's directors, to adopt cost-cutting information technologies to increase productivity, lower labor costs, displace workers, and rationalize production overall.

At the same time, the insertion of the new technologies at one point in the closely interconnected system—locally or nationally—forces their introduction across the entire industrial order. The linkages effected are altering profoundly the character of social existence in its entirety. It is to this development in its most comprehensive sense that we now turn.

AN APPROACH TO A POLITICAL ECONOMY OF CULTURE

To begin to explain *what* is happening in the industrially-advanced Western market economies, and still more importantly, *why* it is happening, requires the exposure and analysis of the sources, mechanics, and dynamics of the new information-based economies. Yet this in itself is not sufficient. It omits alternatives to the electronic developmental course on which the U.S. and other Western economies are embarked. To recognize that there are alternatives, there must be a still more elementary and basic starting point. In my view, it begins with a simple question: *What kind of a society do we want to live in?*

Up to this point in the evolution of human society, this question was not deemed, by those in command, to be a relevant consideration. Choice did not enter into it. Things happened. Economic and technological "imperatives" prevailed. Challenges, and they occurred often, to the prevailing order, generally were ruthlessly suppressed.

Technological change, itself an outcome of complex social forces, was claimed to be an autonomous force. Historically, of course, this was never true. Today, the idea of the neutrality of technology, though still asserted, is less easy to maintain. The institutionalization and capture of science and engineering for deliberate and specific politico-military-economic objectives, by no means only a phenomenon of this century, has been especially marked since the Second World War.[3]

Under these changed circumstances, people and nations are forced, if they wish literally to survive, to act differently than they have in any earlier time. They are compelled to regard technology and its influence on the general direction of social existence, as a subject for public discussion and decision-making, *not* as an external force over which they have no claim or power.

Technology has never been autonomous of the culture in which it developed. Today it constitutes an inseparable part of it. The conscious task of asking what kind of a society is desired, now becomes peoples' only effective response to an otherwise menacing social order, propelled by a technology increasingly removed from public accountability.

Asking this question in the most uncompromising way, and thoroughly examining and discussing the implications of the choices and sentiments expressed, makes it impossible to believe that the conditions that have been reviewed in preceding chapters—the privatization of the public sphere; the militarization of the universe; and the wild jockeying to capture the technological and market lead in the new information technology[4]—are meeting the needs of most people.

Actually, it is now possible for those who want to change things, to grapple with the role of culture in general and its relation to technology and economics in particular. Again, the most unyielding obstacle to such an engagement is the usurpation of the informational system for the maintenance of the transnational corporate order's status quo.

All the same, a meaningful political economy of culture must concern itself, in the first instance, with the overall quality of the social existence that is being created. It must seek to discover the totality of what is happening and to accept no development as being outside the realm of human intervention and, if necessary, resistance.

THE QUALITY OF EXISTENCE IN THE ADVANCED INDUSTRIAL MARKET ECONOMY

In a series of articles, books, and newspaper columns, Jeremy Seabrook has examined Britain's course of social development through the era of industrialization up to the present. Seabrook finds a pervasive "decay of human resources" alongside a massive increase in the production of material goods. Where there is not the ultimate wastage of human beings by under- and unemployment, there is the near-desperate acquisition of commodities as a (totally inadequate) substitute for individual and community "caring relations" and "human solidarity":

> It seems that more and more things are being taken away from people, and sold back in the form of commodities and services. Intangible human attributes are whisked away; and then have to be bought with money: skills, competence, and knowledge. It is the more powerful for being an invisible process, but because it is invisible, and has gone largely unrecorded except in ill-defined feelings, it has to fall back on the rhetoric of absolute poverty, although it is something quite distinct from it...We surrender more and more of our substance, and wait for it to reappear in the market place, where we believe in its values because of the price tag it bears.[5]

Seabrook is describing contemporary Britain but he could just as well be writing about the transformations being effected by electronics, under market conditions, in the United States and elsewhere. In all these changes, the same fundamental issues reappear: what kind of a social order is being created? How do people view themselves and others? Is the social web of human "caring relations" being strengthened or destroyed?

CONSIDERATIONS FOR A POLITICAL ECONOMY OF CULTURE

If, as Alain Madec writes, "informatization is, in fact, and more and more, inseparable from the 'cultural industries' and from the general education of human beings,"[6] it is perilous to ignore the rampaging commercialism now enfolding the new information processes and instrumentation.

No better indication of this condition is available than the report submitted by the Information Technology Advisory Panel to the British Government in 1983.

Leaving no room for misunderstanding, the report is titled: "Making A Business of Information." Its thesis "is that new technology is eroding many of the distinctions that have previously distinguished one form of information medium from another: publications, film, and news services are now all becoming aspects of an expanding 'tradeable information' sector."[7]

The report itself is dedicated to promoting the futher expansion of the commercial information sphere, describing it in a way that exemplifies the process underway.

The highest political leadership in the market economies of the West is thus collaborating with the forceful information hardware and software companies, in recasting the informational system, eliminating its public and social features, and extending its commercial and profitmaking character.

These efforts and the consequences they will have on the general social life of the nation are, or should be, the vibrant subject matter for a powerful and exciting political economy of culture. However, there is no finely wrought theory available to explain the new conditions. Formal economics, from the mid-19th century on, has been occupied with exorcising the influence of Marx. It excludes the political, to say nothing of the cultural, condition from its analysis. At the same time, cultural theorists have been reluctant to acknowledge an economic component in cultural activities, except as a very remote and general background factor, only tenuously related to cultural activity and production.

Yet the separation of culture, politics, and economics is now absurd. Electronic communication provides a common denominator for an ever-growing share of the production of *all* goods and services. And information, which has become an important part of the production process, as well as being a significant good in its own right, is governed too by market criteria which produce uniformities in cultural and industrial production.

For these reasons, Nicholas Garnham insists on the applicability of a general theory of political economy to the developments already observable and those still underway:

> In order to understand the structure of our culture, its production, consumption and reproduction and of the role of the mass media in that process, we increasingly need to confront some of the central questions of political economy in general, the problem of productive and non-productive labor, the relations between the private and public sectors and the role of the State in capitalist accumulation, the role of advertising within late capitalism, etc.[8]

Understanding that the cultural industries today are indispensable to the maintenance of the market economy and, in fact, constitute its vital core, makes it necessary to expand and extend the boundaries of cultural analysis.

Raymond Williams too, writes about these developments, and stresses the necessity of reworking older theoretical formulations, to take into account the modern changes. He emphasizes that the old distinction between the economic "base" and the non-material "superstructure"—the cultural forms and expressions of a given social order—require:

> an especially sharp contemporary correction, since the means of communication as means of social production, and in relation to this the production of the means of communication themselves, have taken on a quite new significance within the generally extended communicative character of modern societies and between modern societies. This can be seen, very strikingly, within the totality of modern economic and "industrial" production, where, in the transport, printing and electronic industries "communicative production" has reached a qualitatively different place in its relation to—more strictly its proportion of—production in general. Moreover, this outstanding development is still at a relatively early stage, and in electronics especially is certain to go very much further.[9]

The changes in the "means of social production," and social reproduction, are especially observable in the educational sphere. The elemental and fundamental processes of education—transmitting the social wisdom and the basic codes and definitions that structure this wisdom—are being altered. The institution of teaching, formal and informal, for example, is being remolded—to specify only a few of the most important pressures—by the information requirements of the high technology corporate sector, the changing structure of the economy, and the application of electronic technologies for classroom cost cutting—that is, reduction of teaching staff.

Yet it is precisely in situations such as this one, that the combination of technological change, economic calculation, and social institutional form have to be seen at their most complex interactional level, affecting the general socio-cultural condition. The direction in which teaching may be pointed is suggestive. It comes not from what might seem to be the causative agent, the new electronic technologies and their remarkably flexible capabilities for the transmission of messages. It comes as well from the *social* utilization of these new forms of instruction and learning.

When, for example, Brown University signs an agreement with IBM, as has Carnegie-Mellon University as well, in which the University receives large amounts of computer equipment and offers in return its faculty's research expertise to assist IBM in product and programming development, new, if not questionable relationships, are being established in American higher education.[10]

Similarly, as private corporations take over, as they are now doing, larger portions of the educative function with electronic techniques, imparted on the job or in specially organized schooling conditions, this cannot be regarded as an inevitable nor necessarily socially desirable, utilization of electronic audiovisual instrumentation. Corporate-provided or administered education issues from specific socio-politico-economic decisions and non-decisions throughout the institutional system.

The new educational formats follow from those instances in which funds are made available or are withheld; where knowledgable personnel are employed because they are adequately paid; where governmental assistance is provided or withheld; where taxes are or are not levied, or even cut; where incentives are offered or withdrawn. In sum, there exists a large array of discrete variables, which in any specific case, combine variously to affect outcomes.

It is in this far from neat, actually, terribly tangled social sphere, that a political economy of culture has to be created. It requires, among other qualities, the scrutiny of decision-making processes, the identification of the participants as far as it is possible to do so, the weighting of their relative influences, and the factoring in of fiscal, administrative, and technical acts of commission and omission.

The domain of work, unlikely as it may seem, is another sphere in which a political economy of culture is best suited to illuminate the processes in motion. For work, as well as instruction, is undergoing great change. How the new technologies are being employed affects greatly not only the availability of jobs, but what actually constitutes the job.

Workers historically, have possessed varying skills. What does the new instrumentation do to these capabilities? Are new skills being acquired by information workers that may be eliminated later along in the information-based economy? Are some workers acquiring greater skills than heretofore while many others experience an accelerating loss of skill—the trend to deskilling that Braverman called attention to in the mid-1970s?[11]

Are changes in the work sites contributing to more or less worker participation in the labor process as well as in the essential routines of daily life? And, are these changes being equally experienced by all or only certain groups in the work force?

If a significant section of the work force is being made redundant, or incapable of participating in the meaningful decisions of existence, the human and economic costs are incalculable. Are the cultural consequences any less grave?

Does it matter to have a work force, for the most part excluded from a meaningful activity and, at the same time, attached to or tending "intelligent" machines? Is this not an economic-technological development that affects the core of human existence?

What may be thought, in this regard, of the increasingly pervasive phenomenon of enormously commercialized sport and spectacle? Does this serve, however unintended, as a social pacifier by which the huge vacuum opening up in the lives of working people is filled? A political economy of culture, of necessity, therefore, examines critically the evolution of the work process and associates it with the *content* of the cultural industries, apart from the equally important task of detailed study of the operation and mechanics of these industries.

THE ROLE OF THE STATE IN THE INFORMATION-BASED ECONOMY

Relating the production process to cultural outcomes constitutes an important part of a political economy of the emerging information-based economy. Yet a useful theory requires still another essential element, the political component, to be capable of its task of providing meaning and guidance. This leads to an examination of the political machinery of advanced capitalism.

Developments and innovations in electronics, and the very creation of the U.S. information-based economy, would have been unrealizable without the continuous, large-scale intervention and assistance of the state. Observable most clearly in the military sector, the basic features of the relationship between government and the new technology repeat themselves in the general electronic developments of the last forty years.

This adds up, in brief, to government-financing of the early research and subsequent technological development, as well as the government supplying the initial, and ample market. Once the process/product has become viable —can be sold at a profit—there is private, corporate takeover of the operational facilities and techniques.

The latest experimental development, the space shuttle, is an exemplary, but in no way exceptional case:

> No attempt will be made to recoup the more than $10 billion in development costs, which are considered an investment in a national resource.

writes the science editor of the *New York Times*. However, the "national resource" sooner or later becomes a *private* resource.

> The space agency. . .is considering several schemes for turning over the ground processing of the shuttle craft to a private contractor. . .Two teams of aerospace companies, one led by Rockwell International and the other by the Lockheed Corporation, are bidding to take over the shuttle ground operations at Kennedy Space Center, probably starting in 1984.[12]

It is often taken for granted that increased scientific knowledge and the practical application of this knowledge, develop in an off-hand, almost random and inadvertent way. Generally, this is an inaccurate description of what happened in the past. It is certainly inapplicable to the present age.

Throughout the second half of the twentieth century, the interventionist practices of the state in the economy overall, and in scientific and technical developments in particular, have been decisive for the emergence of certain broad fields of activity. Less favored areas, of which we hear little, do not get an opportunity to flourish.

The enormous attention of the American media to the Japanese national effort to spur high-tech industries notwithstanding, electronics has been at the head of the list of U.S. government-supported and encouraged fields of inquiry, development, and application. In addition to heavy expenditures funnelled through the military services to the private corporate sector, the scientific and academic communities have been unostentatiously, but quite intentionally, pointed in the same direction with the help of sizable grants. These have had the unsurprising effect of attracting the attention and talent of "pure" and "objective" scientists and scholars. (See Table 1.[13])

The National Science Foundation, for example, in its allocation of government funds, has played a key role in channeling intellectual interest and endeavor to computer-based scholarly and industrial activities.

What this means is that the content, direction, and general tone of scientific academic research have been set from above, whatever the protestations of the scientific community to the contrary. This is true at least within certain limits. It follows that funds are not scarce for studies that support and reinforce the "promise" of computerization, for example. One might look long for and find little of funded research that hypothesizes on the negative effects of computerization, as it is being applied currently.

The state's role in the economy, and especially in the newly emerging information sector, may vary from one market economy to another. Such differences are attributable in part, to historical patterns. More often, they reflect widely different national levels of economic strength, across the economy at large, or in specific industrial branches. Equally important is the strength and level of awareness of the workers' movement in each country. If it is powerful, and at least minimally informed on the matters in hand, the state may well be constrained in its intention to assist capital. Here too, there is room for significant variability in policy in each national setting.

In the United States, in recent years, it has been the vogue to extol the virtues of "deregulation." Allegedly, private industries are liberated from government intervention and control. Actually, this has offered an opportunity to already-powerful companies to take advantage of their strong positions to extract maximum advantage in domestic and international markets, released from any sort of social accountability.

When, for example, AT&T is "deregulated" and thereby enabled to operate without restraint in the international sphere as a data processor and

TABLE 1
COLLEGES AND UNIVERSITIES AMONG THE TOP
500 DEFENSE DEPARTMENT CONTRACTORS, 1982

	Amount of Contracts (add 000)	Rank in top 500
Johns Hopkins University	$235.517	13
Massachusetts Institute of Technology	216.562	18
Illinois Institute of Technology	44.418	43
University of California	35.345	52
Georgia Institute of Technology Research Institute	26.689	63
Stanford University	22.783	73
University of Texas	15.720	86
University of Dayton	13.505	90
Pennsylvania State University	12.254	93
New Mexico State University	11.745	96
University of Washington	10.388	104
Carnegie-Mellon University	10.028	107
University of Southern California	9.854	110
Utah State University	9.431	113
University of Illinois	8.957	118
University of Maryland	7.237	142
University of Rochester	6.976	148
University of New Mexico	6.566	152
Columbia University	5.468	164
California Institute of Technology	5.355	165
Cornell University	4.872	173
Ohio State University Research Foundation	4.674	177
University of Wisconsin	4.611	179
Yale University	4.204	182
University of Michigan	4.095	184
University of Pennsylvania	3.790	194
Georgia Institute of Technology	3.789	195
Oregon State University	3.485	208
University of Arizona	3.450	209
University of Massachusetts	3.433	210
Virginia Polytechnic Institute & State University	3.389	213
Princeton University	2.855	229
Boston College	2.811	231
Florida State University	2.786	232
University of Miami	2.752	236
Oklahoma State University	2.746	237
George Washington University	2.736	238
Harvard University	2.736	239
Boston University	2.702	241
University of Denver	2.635	247
University of Minnesota	2.459	258
Purdue University Research Foundation	2.430	260
University of Utah	2.387	264
New York State University Research	2.314	271
Rensselaer Polytechnic Institute	2.305	272
University of Hawaii	2.214	276

continued

TABLE 1 (continued)

	Amount of Contracts (add 000)	Rank in top 500
Texas A&M University Research Foundation	2.153	279
University of Florida	2.143	280
University of Colorado	2.073	283
Lehigh University	2.034	286
University of Rhode Island	2.018	287
Brown University	1.942	294
Northeastern University	1.920	296
Northwestern University	1.916	297
New York University	1.896	299
University of Pittsburgh	1.817	308
Colorado State University	1.806	310
Case Western Reserve University	1.744	315
Georgetown University	1.730	317
North Carolina State University	1.718	319
University of Iowa	1.703	320
University of North Carolina	1.676	325
New York Polytechnic Institute	1.626	328
Michigan State University	1.619	331
University of Tennessee	1.531	345
Texas Technical University	1.508	347
Stevens Institute of Technology	1.469	358
University of Virginia	1.415	364
Duke University	1.390	368
Wentworth Institute of Technology	1.387	369
New Mexico Institute of Mining and Technology	1.340	374
University of Kansas	1.287	380
Clemson University	1.273	384
University of Connecticut	1.241	389
Michigan Technological University	1.231	391
Drexel University	1.230	393
University of Central Florida	1.132	409
Louisiana State University	1.070	424
Rutgers University	1.024	429
Syracuse University	1.003	437
Howard University	982	441
University of Missouri	963	448
Washington State University	957	449
Emmanuel College (Mass.)	955	450
University of Alabama	917	466
Arizona State University	852	482
Washington University (Mo.)	849	483

transmitter, this is hardly an indication of the withdrawal of governmental support or involvement. It is, in practice, the government's benediction on one of the most powerful American corporations to extend its operations overseas, under the umbrella of U.S. global power.

In other market economies, with less powerful industries, the state, of necessity, assumes a more activist role in promoting the well-being of individual firms or entire industrial sectors.

Yet in either case, the activist or the seemingly passive, the state looks after the perceived needs of the most powerful part of the property-owning class. It does what it can, in national situations that may differ markedly, to advance the interests of that grouping. Indeed, the *national* interest is defined in terms of that powerful fraction. At the same time, the state cannot be indifferent to the expressed demands of the workers' movement in these matters, *if* they are indeed articulated and support is mobilized for their implementation.

Accordingly, a political economy of culture and communication has to take into account national economic, historical, and cultural differences and attempt to explain how these work themselves out in specific state policies and practices.

FROM THE AGGREGATE TO THE INDIVIDUAL

Yet all of these considerations, basic as they are, constitute only a framework, within which individual and group practices produce specific informational and cultural products.

How do the new information technologies, the institutions that are created to employ and administer them, and the governmental policies that are promulgated to strengthen national ownership groups, sort themselves out to eventually influence cultural outputs and the general condition of individual lives? More specifically, how do these largescale social forces influence the *content* of the huge volume of general message-making that characterizes an industrially-developed society? This is the question that relentlessly confronts a political economy of culture and for which answers, despite great complexity, have to be sought.

Some believe that the changed conditions in advanced capitalism require a loosening of the older, supposedly direct, material links that were believed to bind inexorably the work of artists, writers, jurists, scientists, and intellectuals to the specific needs and interests of the dominating class. The idea of "determination" is relaxed in this reading of developments, and the setting of limits is considered more appropriate.

Yet it may be that the developments in the computerization of the economy suggest a different conclusion, or, at least one that puts greater weight on the fundamental shift in what constitutes the "base" of the economy.

If commercial production and sale of information are on the way to becoming dominant features of the economy that is emerging, and if they are creating a convergence between cultural and industrial production in general, the conditions that bind the cultural/communications sphere to the institutional infrastructure *may be tightening* rather than loosening.

The ascendancy of commercialized information in all kinds of productive activity, may make for less, not more autonomy, in creative as well as routine work. Despite this not improbable outcome, efforts to push the concept of "determinancy" toward the idea of "limits" and "boundaries" may be helpful in understanding the wave of information policy-making sweeping across Western Europe and North America.

When a governmentally-appointed special commission, in the Fall of 1982, for example, proposed the rapid development of cable television in the United Kingdom, it matter-of-factly ruled out the option of a publicly-owned and operated system, stating flatly that:

> the national common carrier model appears unlikely as it is inconsistent with the Government's policy of competition and its expressed view that cabling should not make significant demands on public expenditure.[14]

In this instance, the limits that were imposed are indirect, but no less confining. They set the basic direction of a powerful medium far into the future. The mechanics of how these limits operate deserve brief amplification.

The simple and arbitrary expression of preference for a privately-owned cable system *also predetermined,* at the same time, its source of revenues—advertising. In fact, the Commission was optimistic about a general growth in overall advertising that would accompany a privatized cable system:

> We find it difficult to believe that advertising revenue is fixed at its present level in real terms and that advertising on cable would necessarily mean the same size cake being sliced more thinly.[15]

What the Commission in fact proposed and anticipated, clearly, was a significant increase of advertising in the United Kingdom. This, it was expected would finance the new system and return profits to the investors.

Should these recommendations be followed, and, if the Commission is correct in its revenue estimates—admittedly an "iffy" situation—a striking example is provided of the limits that economic decisions impose on cultural creation. The most obvious cultural consequence is that a decision has been made, however unwitting, to further saturate the British viewing public with transnational corporate programming and advertising.

This occurs because it is primarily only within the capability of the huge American media combines to provide the programming that the new facilities in the U.K. (and across Western Europe, in general) require to operate efficiently and profitably. "In order to fill the channels created by cable and direct satellite broadcasting [in the U.K.]," notes one report, "a variety of program services is being assembled. In addition to Home Box Office [TIME, Inc.], a consortium of four major British companies has aligned with MGM/UA, Paramount, and Universal Pictures to provide a 12-hour-daily subscription movie service in the spring."[16]

This is only the beginning of the parade. American firms have been buying into European equipment and production companies to acquire continental outlets for their goods and services.[17] TIME, Inc. and Warner Communications have been especially active. With the arrival of U.S. equipment and programming, the transnational sponsor cannot be far behind.

To be sure, development of cable as a private investment opportunity is not limited to the U.K. The United States has the distinction, such as it is, of "pioneering" this direction. Though cable is still in its relative infancy, the private ownership of a potentially remarkable *public* technology, already, has seriously limited, if not permanently injured, the development and expansion of its public use.[18]

These, then, are the underlying conditions, the limits that situate the eventual outcomes. This said, there is still considerable space remaining for the play of creative effort. How that expresses itself is surely an important additional area for study and analysis. But the transcendental condition is the commercial limit and all the constraints it brings in its trail.

SETTING LIMITS IN THE INTERNATIONAL SPHERE

At the international level, limits also are set in which technico-economic arrangements prefigure the subsequent informational-cultural activity.

If consortia of powerful transnational corporations, for example, are successful in establishing private, international communication networks via satellites and, at the same time, if national broadcasting and telecommunications structures (the PTTs) are weakened, the consequences go well beyond engineering and economics.

The private consortia, accountable only to security analysts' review of their balance sheets, will be, in effect, the primary agents in molding and shaping the rapidly growing spheres of information generation, processing, transmission, and dissemination. These seemingly technical activities, bear heavily on the overall cultural atmosphere of the societies involved.

Pierre Dreyfus, at one time advisor to former President Giscard d'Estaing, explains this:

> There is a tremendous potential for cultural exchanges even cultural domination, through computer technology. Let us consider computer models. Would

it be credible for an American banker to consult a Soviet based economic model? Even if it were in an area where the Soviets have done good work and established a good model, which they certainly have. We would not use such a model because we would think it was biased. *But we are doing the same thing to the rest of the world. We are giving them our models and they have to process their data through our models, which means that in a way we are changing their cultural mode.*[19]

Admittedly, there will be variations from one locale to another. Specific national circumstances—historical, geographical, developmental, and the class structure—will combine differently in the final outcomes. Despite these conditions of national exceptionality, however, there will also be some overarching uniformities.

The current movement toward the privatization of national communication structures, alongside the growing strength of private transnational communications, can be expected to produce information systems adhering to market, ability-to-pay criteria. Information and data may be of a quality hitherto unimagined in richness, but their availability will be affected by a selection process unfailingly tied to the wealth and income of the user.

These, in fact, are the already observable conditions in the United States, where the process is most advanced. Basic information, freely available to the general public, is disappearing. The stockpile of social information is being privately appropriated and sold to those who can pay for it.[20] Since United States corporate information combines operate globally, the privatization of information systems proceeds internationally, though not without some resistance of labor and/or national rival capitals.

Actually, the vital connections between technico-economic and cultural affairs have been appreciated for some time, at least as early as the 1960s, in the international community. The demand of the 125 or more less-industrialized nations for a new international economic order, and later, a new international information order, has contained as well, a strong cultural awareness, expressed in an insistence on national cultural sovereignty.

Actually, the international debates and negotiations over space, law of the sea, radio frequency spectrum allocation and information have reflected an increasing understanding by a good part of the world, that economic and technological questions are, at the same time, informational and cultural issues. A report about telecommunications, prepared for the United States Congress, takes note of this development.

Besides lamenting the appearance of a relatively recently-established majority of poor nations, whose interests increasingly collide with those of the United States' private corporate sector, it is acknowledged that:

There has been a gradual shift toward recognizing the legitimacy of nontechnical factors such as political and cultural interests and values in ITU [International Telecommunications Union] deliberations and in other international forums.[21]

As reliance on technology and economic strength has been the mainstay of American world power in the 20th century, it has been important, in the application of that power against weaker states, that as little attention as possible be paid to the mechanics and context of its operation. Thus, the claim of neutrality of technology and the impartiality of the world market (and the law of comparative advantage) were and remain essential doctrines of American global power.

It is hardly surprising therefore, that any demonstration of the indivisibility of technology, economics, politics, and culture is anathema to American decision-making centers. When international bodies such as UNESCO are stigmatized by U.S. leaders as being "politicized," it is because they have in some way or other, recognized or acted upon this inseparability.

It is neither whimsey nor ignorance on the part of United States leadership to rebuke and punish any such manifestation, for it clearly weakens the central pillars of American imperial control. For this reason, a political economy of culture cannot expect to receive a warm welcome in the command centers—academic, governmental, or corporate—of the U.S. economy.

Still, the forces that are moving communication and culture to the center of the information economy, and making them primary agents of production are pushing ahead relentlessly, propelled by competition and crisis. Communication and culture assume a central position in a rapidly changing economy while the institutional envelope of private ownership and market criteria remains intact, and indeed, largely determining. It is in this remarkably contradictory situation, of rapid technico-social change alongside old forms of control and decision-making, that a political economy of culture assumes its new significance. Nothing less than the questions of how we live and, how we want to live, have become the starting points for analysis.

NOTES TO CHAPTER FIVE

1.   "Quatre Cents Intellectuels En Sorbonne," *Le Monde,* February 15, 1983.
2.   The *New York Times,* September 17, 1982.
3.   Daniel Deudney, *Whole Earth Security: A Geopolitics of Peace,* Worldwatch Paper 55, July, 1983.
4.   Ruth Davis, former director of the National Bureau of Standards' Institute for Computer Sciences and Technology, explained why the United States must pursue the quest for a super-computer: "We're losing sight of the fact that we need super-computing for entirely different objectives than technology...The race we're really in is between countries, not for supercomputers, not for national security...We're in a race to control the resources of the world, both

natural resources and information resources." Jake Kirchner, "Supercomputing Seen Key to Economic Success," *Computerworld,* October 3, 1981, p. 8.

5. Jeremy Seabrook, "Poverty As Metaphor—or Why both Peter and Paul Feel Robbed," *New Society,* February 28, 1980, pp. 439–441.

6. Alain Madec, "Les Flux Transfrontieres de donnees," *La Documentation Francaise,* Paris, 1982, p. 19.

7. "Making A Business of Information," A Report by the Information Technology Advisory Panel, Cabinet Office, London, Her Majesty's Stationery Office, September 1983, p. 11.

8. Nicholas Garnham, "Contribution to a Political Economy of Mass Communication," *Media, Culture and Society,* Vol. No. 2, 1979, p. 145.

9. Raymond Williams, "Means of Communication As Means of Production," *Problems In Materialism and Culture,* Verso and NLB, 1980, p. 53.

10. "Brown and IBM Plan A 3-Year Computer Project," The *New York Times,* November 13, 1983; also, Richard M. Cyert, "Personal Computing in Education and Research," *Science* (editorial), November 11, 1983, Vol. 222, No. 4624.

11. Harry Braverman, "Labor and Monopoly Capital," *Monthly Review Press,* New York, 1974.

12. John Noble Wilford, "NASA Wants Corporations To Help Pay The Freight," The *New York Times,* November 14, 1982 (*News of the Week*).

13. Source: U.S. Department of Defense.

14. Report of the Inquiry Into Cable Expansion and Broadcasting Policy, Chairman Lord Hunt of Tamorth, London, HMSO, October, 1982, Command 8679.

15. *Ibid.,* p. 13.

16. Sally Bedell Smith, "Pay-TV Services Are Planned for Britain in 1984," The *New York Times,* December 29, 1983.

17. John Tagliabue, "Wiring Europe for Cable TV," The *New York Times,* June 25, 1983.

18. Peter Kerr, "Study Says Cable Channel Use Low," The *New York Times,* January 12, 1984, and Sally Bedell Smith, "Reduced Cable-TV Plan Sought in Milwaukee," The *New York Times,* January 13, 1984.

19. Pierre Dreyfus, "Cultural Differences and Information Technology," Reprinted in *TDR,* Vol. 7, No. 8, December, 1983, p. 458.

20. "Librarians Warn of Mounting Threat to Government Information," News release, American Library Association, Chicago, October, 1982.

21. *Radio Frequency Use and Management: Impacts from the World Administrative Radio Conference of 1979, Summary,* Congress of the United States, Washington, D.C. Office of Technology Assessment, 1981.

Chapter Six

Paradoxes of the Information Age

The far reaching shifts in the United States and international economies are having a profound impact on the lives of tens of millions of Americans. What is being produced, the conditions of the work place, the education of the people, and the quality of personal life are undergoing massive changes. And more may be expected!

The forces promoting these changes are diverse and complex but two of them are central, initiatory, and interactive. One, is the full blown emergence of the transnational corporation, carrying on its business in many locales around the world. The other is the new information technologies and processes that have qualitatively altered the ways in which information and data are generated, processed, stored, retrieved, and disseminated.

Actually, the scale of activity of the transnational corporation is unthinkable without the new information technologies. At the same time, these technologies have found their main application and utilization in the administrative, productive, and marketing operations of large scale, transnational firms. To be sure, there are other major employers of advanced communications systems. There are the military and government. Both of these heavy users, however, have as their primary task the protection and/or representation of the transnational corporation.

The new international division of labor now being created by the employment of the new information technologies is not yet fully matured. The export of capital, new investment patterns, and the relocation of production continue to produce shock waves throughout the international system. All the same, some generalizations may be made about what is still in the process of formation. These may best be formulated as paradoxes, as contradictory developments that at first seem to make one outcome inevitable, but, on close scrutiny, suggest an entirely different conclusion.

The paradoxes outlined here do not exhaust the range of possibilities that the present changes are producing. Still, they may serve as a starting point for further analysis and as a recapitulation of the major themes in this book.

THE RENEWAL OF DYNAMISM ALONGSIDE INCREASED SYSTEMIC VULNERABILITY

The new information technologies have provided a tremendous stimulus to capitalism. Nationally and internationally, the system has been invigorated in a number of ways. Most directly, there has been a dramatic spurt in what are called the high-technology industries. Computer manufacturing, telecommunications, data processing, information storage, retrieval, and dissemination, and automated equipment are high growth sectors.

New facilities and industrial complexes have appeared in various parts of the country. Significant numbers of workers, professionals, and managers have found jobs in the new fields. And, if the information goods and services component is not comparable as an economic force to the automobile and its related industries, it is still in its relative infancy.

But perhaps more important than the direct impact on economic activity, significant as this is, the new information technologies have facilitated an enormous shift in the balance of power between capital and labor, to the advantage of the former.

The communications supplied by satellites hooked to computers, have enabled the transnational corporation to move boldly across the national and international stage. The big, internationally active companies now have the means to shift production sites, switch capital investment, and move international exchange rapidly and sometimes instantaneously. Capital now moves routinely on a global scale. Labor remains a national, if not a locally bound factor of production. As a consequence, national labor forces are, if not entirely, increasingly subject to capital's capability to relocate if its demands are not acceded to.

In Scotland, for example, this capability of transnational capital is called the "Hyster factor," and refers to the "take it or leave it" offer to the 500 workers at the Hyster company's forklift truck factory at Irvine, in Ayrshire. They were told recently that the company (a U.S. transnational headquartered in Portland, Oregon) would pull out of Scotland if they did not accept a 10 percent pay cut.[1] The workers, with only 11 workers voting "no," accepted.

How duplicitous as well as brutal is the exercise of this new power of transnational capital, and how helpless labor is before it, is indicated in still another account, this one in an American newspaper, on the behavior of the Hyster Co.:

Hyster's workers in Irvine have no union. The vote might have been no different if they did. The most muscular union in Europe isn't a match for a company run out of a place like Portland. A union is concerned with the workers in its country; a multinational knows no bounds. While the chief executive can look to the far corners of his realm through the screen of a desk-top terminal, the unionist still hesitates to make an international phone call. While a shop steward dickers with a plant manager, the plant's destiny may be determined on another continent.

How one group of workers in one country (or locale) can be played off against another, is described in the same report:

Plant managers within a multinational company could easily tell their Swiss workers, as the managers of one reputedly did, that new work was going to the lower-paid British; tell the British that production was being passed to the more efficient French; and tell the French it was creating jobs for the highly cooperative Swiss. *Companies rarely tell their scattered workers everything. Workers of different nationalities rarely tell each other anything. In an age when information is power, they lack both.* [2]

And, as if these enhanced capabilities were not enough, the availability of powerful global communications networks, enables the big firms to penetrate national and world markets formerly inaccessible.

For these and other reasons, many of the stagnation theories of capitalism, which abounded in the 1930s and early 1940s, quite justifiably, have been mothballed. Dynamism and growth along with some sectoral decay, seem more appropriate descriptors of the current scene. But the picture is not a complete one.

While capitalism admittedly is enjoying a new burst of energy, its room for maneuver narrows steadily. The complete dependence of the central force in modern capitalism, the transnational corporation, on unimpeded international communication, requires a relatively secure world system of stable nation states. This is the least likely outcome of the forces now in motion, actively stimulated by the renewed energies of high-tech capitalism. A second paradox explains this more fully.

CONSUMERISM AND THE (TEMPORARY) WITHERING OF RADICAL CONSCIOUSNESS

Capitalism has achieved remarkable popular support with its fostering of consumerism. It has sold successfully, a way of life and a set of beliefs, that tie human well-being to the individual possession of an ever-expanding array of purchasable goods and services. Acquiring material goods has either superceded, or been made the equivalent, of love, friendship, and community.

In the highly industrialized market economies, people have widely accepted this ethic, however much they may disavow it in public conversation. To a very considerable extent, the inability of radical movements in Western Europe to change decisively the political and economic structures of their societies, is explained by the unwillingness of a majority of people to engage in activities that threaten either the possession of, or the hope of acquiring consumer goods and perquisites. It is evidently felt, whether articulated or not, that literally nothing is worth losing the opportunity to get, or to hold on to, consumer goods.

Accepted as well, by a dominant fraction of the population in the North Atlantic region, is the linkage of consumption to democracy. Consumer choice here is equated with meaningful politico-economic choice. Shopping in a supermarket, with its crowded shelves of products is, in this perspective, a democratic practice.

The intense drilling of the people to participate in the consumer society is facilitated greatly, if it is not directly motivated, by advertising, which saturates most information channels—especially in the United States. The newest information technologies, which have many, and sometimes contradictory applications, as they are now being utilized, substantially increase the penetrative power of the marketing system. Interactive, two-way television, for example, still in its early development, is seen largely as a home marketing technology.

From all this, it seems reasonable to conclude that the individualist, possessive ethic has triumphed, in the short run at least, in the heartlands of capitalist enterprise. The system itself is stronger than ever on account of this. Though not eliminated, radical, equalitarian impulses have been weakened greatly, and alternative conceptions of life in an industrial world are, for the moment, unable to attract support, or bleaker still, unable to be conceptualized.

Yet here, too, the situation is hardly stabilized. In the developed market economies, the strength of a "democracy of consumption," rests almost entirely on economic growth and, at a minimum, on shares for all in an enlarging economic pie. If growth cannot be maintained, the consumerist ethos falters. Indeed, it is likely to become a source of growing dissatisfaction.

As the consumerist economies rely heavily on mass media advertising to keep demand high, there is a built-in, potentially disruptive force continuously at work, either, when the economic engine begins to stall, or if the resource availabilities begin to contract. A Club of Rome study touches on the second of these possibilities: ". . . economic policies based on quantitative growth through the stimulation of consumption will hardly prove effective in an era of resource limitation. . . ."[3]

If this is so in the already industrialized states, the condition is still more aggravated in the Third World, where large numbers of people live close to, or sometimes fall below, the margin of survival. In these regions, now being integrated rapidly into the world market system of transnational enterprise by the new information technologies, the paradox is striking.

The information systems in most of the nations in the less industrialized world are being transformed into marketing networks for the resident transnational corporations. Increasingly, advertising-supported television carries the consumption messages of the world business system. Additionally, local banking, industrial, transport, and tourist sectors are being connected to the metropolitan informational circuits of the TNCs.

Local elites and the new professional classes quickly accept and embrace the consumerist message. They are also in a position to act on it. For the rest of the population, the overwhelming majority, the effects are less satisfactory. Unable to participate, the artifacts and stimuli of consumerism surround them. At the same time, the character of the economy is distorted to enable a relatively small number of people to enjoy Western consumption standards, while actually diminishing the output of vitally required goods.

Natural resources, on a global scale, are being plundered for a mode of consumption that embodies wastefulness and inequality. The consumerist model, carried into the world at large is, therefore, a radicalizing force, swallowing up irreplaceable natural resources and simultaneously feeding and thwarting human expectations. Political stability is diminished therefore, in proportion to the speed with which the marketing system and its advertising component are extended to the still-impoverished parts of the world.

Installing itself in all corners of the globe, and spreading the message of consumption through its advertising-supported media channels, the transnational corporation is promoting what it most fears, future massive political instability.

THE NEW INFORMATION TECHNOLOGIES CONFRONT NATIONAL SOVEREIGNTY

Domestically and internationally, governance is being changed radically by the availability of the new information technologies. Internationally, the very basis of national sovereignty, for a majority of states, is threatened. A combination of developments, utilizing satellite communications and the linkage of computers, directly undercut national jurisdictions. Remote sensing, for example—scanning a territory with powerful sensors attached to orbiting satellites—routinely maps the globe, obtaining all sorts of resource information without requiring the permission of the scanned region's government. The recipients of this information, moreover, are generally the power centers in the few industrialized countries that possess the technical capability to interpret and to take advantage of the data.

Along with remote sensing, direct satellite broadcasting is now at hand, offering the capability of transmitting messages from the satellite to receivers across the earth, irrespective of national boundaries. Most important of all the new developments, electronic transborder data flows now move in great volume across frontiers, silently and invisibly, transferring data, mostly *within* the transnational corporation's many branches, without oversight or accountability to national authorities.

Unless counter measures are adopted, these developments, taken together, herald the demise of most nation-states, at least as effective control agents of their own national space.

As there is no world government waiting to assume global responsibilities, these developments also suggest the enhanced power of a few superstates who exercise these technical capacities, and a still greater influence of already powerful transnational corporations. In short, the erosion of national sovereignty appears to offer still further reinforcement to the world business system. Thus, the devastating impact of the new technologies on national political organization redounds to the benefit of capitalist enterprise.

But here, too, appearances may be deceptive. The anti-imperialist struggles of the twentieth century are too recent to have been expunged from popular consciousness. Genuine national independence and sovereignty, though hardly (fully) attained by most countries, despite ceremonial trappings of flags and airlines, remain powerful aspirations. The new technological threats to national sovereignty can only rally great oppositional force —already observable in international negotiations over issues such as access to the geostationary orbit, radio frequency allocation, data flow regulation, and the right of nations to control the messages coming into their national space ("prior consent").

American policymakers are not entirely unaware of this opposition. This is discreetly, if indirectly admitted, by George Shultz, Secretary of State: "...the evolution of communication and information technology and its international significance makes it a foreign policy concern of the first magnitude since the ultimate course of communication and information can affect every dimension of our foreign relations...."[4]

There is a domestic equivalent to this dialectic, one with more menacing implications. In the United States, where these developments are most advanced, and therefore most observable, the new information technologies are also deeply affecting the character and role of the national state. In this instance, the impacts also are contradictory.

The new information technologies, for one thing, have contributed greatly to the weakening of the public sector by increasing the profit-making potential of a large number of activities which formerly were non-profitable. Education, health, welfare, and public service functions (and public utilities in Western Europe), fall into this category. The advent of computers and the growth of the information sector in general, have transformed information into a saleable good and encourage many former public service activities to be contracted out for profit. To be sure, factors other than computerization and sale of information are involved in these developments, but nonetheless their contribution to privatization cannot be minimized.

In any case, the trends toward a diminishing public sector in the United States and the United Kingdom are very evident. Yet while public service activities increasingly are privatized, the state's power and role by no means declines correspondingly. It shifts instead toward social control, surveillance, and coercion. In the U.K. and the U.S.A., as national educational and health expenditures contract, military, law enforcement, intelligence, and police outlays expand.

In the high-tech economy, a weak public sector is "balanced" by a strong state, availing itself of the most up-to-date communication instrumentation to maintain social equilibrium alongside grievous economic deterioration for increasing numbers of working people. In the developed market economies, in this time of unrelenting crisis, the state is divested, as much as possible of its welfare function, while it strengthens its coercive capability to handle potentially unruly domestic groupings and perceived (fabricated?) international adversaries.

Not everyone however, agrees with this strategy. Some point out that the problems created by the new technologies can only be met with *increased* government intervention to protect the weaker sections of the population. Charles Lecht, writing about the catastrophic lay-offs made by AT&T, for example, states:

> This is no time for our government to remove itself from the scene, whether it does so in the name of some ideology or of exhaustion of its moral/material resources, while the contesting parties struggle to work things out on their own. Short of instituting its own welfare system, A.T.&T. is powerless to solve the problems of its legion of new ex-employees. It cannot even promise job security to many of its remaining white-collar personnel.[5]

This view goes unattended in the current U.K. and U.S. administrations.

In the poorer lands the situation is reversed. The State is called upon to protect the national patrimony against the TNC's greatly expanded powers provided by the new communications capability to bypass national authority. Yet in both instances, different as they are, the communication technologies are being employed *against* human needs and aspirations.

INFORMATION IMPOVERISHMENT ACCOMPANIES
INFORMATION ABUNDANCE

Satellites, computers, and cable make possible a qualitatively new level of information availability. The present capacity to generate, process, store, retrieve, and disseminate information now exceeds, whatever their extravagance, earlier Utopian visions. Viewed exclusively as a technological capability, it is hardly unrealistic to regard the present situation as one of potential unprecedented abundance and richness of information.

It seems all the more shocking therefore, to acknowledge at the same time, the deepening division of the society into informationally-privileged and informationally-impoverished sectors. What accounts for this?

Above all, the responsibility rests with the social arrangements that are governing the development, utilization, and distribution of the new information technologies and their products. The private firms and institutions that are organizing the new information age are, as a matter of course, making information a merchandisable good, a commodity produced for profit and sale. Specifically, there are companies which design the systems, manufacture the hardware and the software, process the data, create the data bases, and transmit the messages. These and other activities create a new and expanding information sector of the economy.

From the time of Gutenberg, and even before, information production has been controlled and has led to social stratification based on unequal access. What is of special significance about the current situation, is the centrality of information in all spheres of material production, as well as its increasing prominence throughout the economy. Today, information increasingly serves as a primary factor in production, distribution, administration, work, and leisure.

For these reasons, how information itself is produced and made available become crucial determinants affecting the organization of the overall social system.

Largely as a consequence of its heightened value and importance to the entire economy, information is being privatized at an accelerating rate. As we have noted, public sector information functions are being curtailed to facilitate private expansion in this area. Where the public information functions continue to exist, they are brought into the commercial sphere and are compelled to adopt market principles in their operation.

Libraries, for example, though remaining public institutions, introduce computer services and then levy user charges, breaking with longstanding traditions of "free" service. Similarly, the U.S. public mail service is being dismembered though no public official will acknowledge this. However, as large corporations adopt private electronic communication systems and abandon the public mails, costs to *individual* users rise rapidly and services begin to be curtailed as demand falls in response to the increased costs.

Throughout the economy, the privatization and commoditization of information are being accompanied by commercial charges that separate and stratify users by their ability to pay. What hypothetically could be a truly information-rich society, is on the way to becoming a community divided into information "haves" and "have-nots." Across the information spectrum, the evidence of inequality of access, determined by income differentials, multiplies.

The commercialization of information knows no bounds. No source is exempt from the privatization wave, especially as the state's authority is put heavily on the side of the privatizers. And so, there is the spectacle of information deprivation developing in the midst of information abundance.

Is this a reversible development? The answer rests partly in the political process. Sufficient popular mobilization/demand for information access and for protection against rising information costs—higher telephone bills, for instance—*might* arrest these trends. The problem is the familiar one. How can the issue be made understandable, in all its aspects, to impel popular involvement, when the channels of communication remain at the disposal, almost exclusively, of those benefiting most from current policies?

There is yet another dimension to the information gap now widening. This is that the overall pool of information will contract eventually as access and availability become almost entirely tied to an ability-to-pay standard. Increasingly, certain kinds of social information just won't be produced, stored, indexed, or available, for there will be no ready market for it. Yet in a highly inter-dependent industrial economy, the absence of such information can become a grave source of vulnerability to the functioning of the social order.

This outcome, however, will occur, if it does, only in the longterm future. It cannot be expected to influence near-term developments.

THE DISAPPEARANCE OF ORGANIZED LABOR REMOVES A POWERFUL SYSTEM STABILIZER

The new information technologies that provide the transnational corporation with greatly enhanced operational flexibility, locally and globally, have recast as well the historic balance between capital and labor.

Though the labor movement at its most organized and disciplined, has never actually enjoyed an equal position with capital, it has, in several countries, including the United States, won considerable leverage. Until recently, it was capable of defending *some* of its interests, and sometimes advancing them.

For the moment, and perhaps for a long time to come, labor's capability to act as a check on capital and as a defender of its material interests, has been weakened to the point of marginality. The great corporations, domestically and internationally, now have the means to make labor accept their terms, in ways almost unparalleled since the early days of the industrial revolution.

The giant firms, in their ability to shift capital, production, and investment, globally and nationally, have overturned the already less than rough balance exerted by formerly strong, national labor movements. Capital, in its transnational corporate organizational form, is now structurally and operationally thoroughly international. Labor remains local, nationally effective at best.

In these changed circumstances, the era of rising real wages for the industrial work force has come to a halt. Workers now are expected to grant "give backs"—the return of benefits won through decades of social struggle. The very existence of unionism is threatened. In the United States and Britain and elsewhere, the older "smokestack" industries were the strongholds of labor organization. It is these industries that are being "exported" and their work forces left to scrounge for jobs or hand-outs.

At the same time, the new high-tech industries have been singularly successful in avoiding, preventing(?) unionization. "Near Boston," according to one account, "where a proliferation of high technology companies has created tens of thousands of new jobs since 1975, not one of the 133 companies that belong to the Massachusetts High Technology Council is unionized."[6]

The white collar worker and open collar professional have been imbued from earliest schooling with an individualist, anti-labor organizational ethic. Added to this, the new technologies are being utilized, in some cases, to restore patterns of home work and piece work. These further atomize the labor force and interfere with its organization.

While the old industrial centers of unionization shut down, the new complexes of high-tech activity move to locales long resistant to labor organization. In these new centers, the awareness of capital's mobility serves as a continuous warning to the unorganized labor force that it develops solidarity at its peril.

As if these were not problems enough for labor, the new media technologies are being employed to provide an ideological assault on independent worker organization. Increasingly, the big companies, whatever their main industrial activities, engage in direct media production, taking advantage of video and film to manufacture anti-union messages for in-house and national audiences.

These efforts join with corporate advertising, which continues to blanket the commercial media system. Throughout the range of sound and visual imagery, with the limited exception of some popular (rock) music, the ideology of property, individualism, and consumerism prevail. The cultural sphere of the mass media is a realm in which the labor movement and values of human solidarity have no place.[7]

However lamentable, it appears that in the most advanced centers of industrialization, the historic working class movement is being ground down and worn away. Capital's dream of (either) a nonorganized labor force, or production entirely without workers, seems on the way to fulfillment. Marx seemingly has been confounded. It is not the "expropriation of the expropriators" that is happening but the liquidation of the proletariat.

Whether it will come to this is not yet totally clear. What is certain is that the extent to which these developments do occur, and labor as an organized social force largely disappears, capital's dream may well turn out to be its nightmare.

Though rarely acknowledged, the labor movements in the developed market economies, have provided, against capital's will to be sure, a powerful stabilizer, economically and politically, for the market system. Economically, mass purchasing power has been sustained and broadened, assuring a market for a good part of the rising output of the industrial system. Though labor's share of the economic pie has remained remarkably steady over the decades, it has been maintained and somewhat expanded.

Without the ever present claim of organized labor, the intensity of cyclical crisis—never far away—might have been stronger and could have wrought great havoc in the system. On the political side, the existence of an organized labor force, intent on joining electoral coalitions in the United States and presenting its own reformist platform in the U.K. and elsewhere, went a long way in extinguishing radical fires and revolutionary changes during capitalism's most exploitative period of growth and maturation.

Throughout the twentieth century, with few exceptions, organized labor has been a conservative force, often, if that is imaginable, as opposed to radical restructuring of the social order as capital itself. Unions have diminished some of capital's prerogatives, but the ultimate costs to capital have been readily sustainable, because the end result was systemic stabilization.

It is the stabilizing function that now is being removed in the shift to high technologies and an information-based economy. It is quite possible that new forms of labor organization may develop, mobilized around new kinds of issues, not all of which may be totally work-site based. If this does in fact occur, the labor-capital struggle will move to new ground with unpredictable outcomes.

However, if the information-based economy continues to resist unionization successfully, it is difficult at this point to see what social grouping can be called upon to provide the income stabilizing and political defusing function of the old labor movement.

This then is the paradox! Capitalism without organized labor may become a capitalism of political gyrations and persistent and intense economic slump. In the economic sphere, one question alone emphasizes the growing dilemma. Where will the consumer purchasing power come from, as automation bites deeper in the work force and as rising productivity increases the capacity to turn out more goods and services with fewer hands? The authors of the Club of Rome study, *Micro-Electronics and Society,* face the issue squarely: "At the heart of the matter," they write, "is the question of employment." But, "there is the danger that against the background of economic crisis and high unemployment, the rationalization possibilities brought about by technological change will be pursued to the exclusion of all else...."[8]

In other words, left to its own dynamic, capitalism will pursue profits before full employment. In doing so, by means of cost-cutting, the number of jobless will increase.

Where then will the pressure come from to redistribute income, lacking a strongly organized work force? And, if there is no redistribution, or not enough to matter, can moderation continue to prevail in the political sphere?

SHORT-RUN ECONOMIC DECISIONS
AND LONG-RUN CULTURAL CONSEQUENCES

The introduction of cable television, the use of communication satellites, and the pellmell rush into computerization repeat a pattern of technological invention and utilization that appeared early in the history of communication technologies. Whatever differences that there may be today are accountable largely to the enormous concentration of capital that now characterizes the industrial system in general, and the high-tech communication industries in particular.

The construction and launching of a communication satellite, for example, are multi-million dollar ventures, and these exclude the initial costs of research, development, and experimentation. The outlays for cabling a metropolitan area are even more substantial. The manufacture of computers and the creation of computer/telecommunication networks are the exclusive preserves of a handful of giant firms or governments.

This being the material reality of modern communications, the decision-making authority on whether to proceed with any or all of these new technologies, is vested in few hands, all of which are mostly, if not exclusively, responsive to the calculus of immediate economic benefit: profits foremost, and industrial primacy not far behind. When governments are engaged in the process, their concerns are also economic and they center largely around economic growth rates and providing jobs.

In the United States, the United Kingdom, West Germany, France, Canada, Japan, and a few other market economies, the readiness to promote the new communication technologies arises from a combination of motives, varying from one economy to another, but all sharing a short-term economic emphasis. With the possible exception of France—and this must be seen only as a tentative qualification—the consequences of following near-term objectives—profits and jobs—promise to produce far-reaching though longer term destabilizing cultural consequences.

The United States must be seen as exceptional at the same time as it is perhaps the most susceptible to the longer term destabilization forces released by the new technologies. Yet in the time immediately ahead it is difficult not to believe that the U.S. economy, or at least some sectors of it, will derive significant benefits from the widespread adoption domestically and internationally, of the new communications instrumentation and processes.

Already the center of the global information system, America's media products and informational goods cannot fail to gain still greater advantage in the world market. The economies of scale available to U.S. producers who have a huge internal market at their disposal, make the prices of their outputs unmatchable, for the most part, in the international market. This is particularly observable in TV programming but it applies elsewhere.

One result of this phenomenon will be a further increase of American media messages and imagery in national communication circuits in Western Europe, and, more pronouncedly still, in the vast, less-industrialized peripheral areas of the world. So, while West European and other market economies are launching high-tech promotions to stimulate production, create jobs, and grab a chunk of the international market, they are, in fact, opening their societies still further to the advances of the transnational corporations. The TNC's rapidly utilize for their own purposes, the new communications infrastructure ostensibly established to improve national authority. Accordingly, further economic distortions as well as popular frustration, may be expected to intensify throughout these regions.

Domestically, the greatly expanded number of options for receiving information, of necessity will require a continuing escalation of user charges and a consequent accelerated widening of the societal knowledge gap. What some describe as the "Technologies of Freedom"[9] are rapidly becoming the basis for a thoroughly stratified nation.

Increasingly employed for marketing and monitoring, the new communication facilities constitute the infrastructure for an aggressive program of "law and order," aimed at checking any signs of popular discontent. While personal computers are being sold to the public as freedom-enhancing and self-enriching instruments, the multiplying distress signals in the economy are making it less and less likely for solutions to be found on an individual basis.

All the same, national leaderships in the West, with unfailing media support, encourage the belief that the new information technologies are essential to deliver information abundance as well as escape the hardships of economic crisis.

Still, this good news is received with some skepticism by many people. For this reason, there is concern at policy-making levels that the new information technology may begin to suffer the fate of nuclear power, which now is greatly feared by wide sectors of the population. Care must be taken, therefore, to consolidate in the general public, a favorable impression of information technology. An Organization of Economic Cooperation and Development (OECD) proposal for an international conference on information, trade, and communication services, makes this concern explicit:

> The ultimate aim of the conference would be to...make sure that the social consensus on the benefits of information technology continues unabashed in the years to come....There is a certain danger that information technology might increasingly be regarded as a scare technology like nuclear technology; the conference might contribute to avoiding this potentially negative feeling in various strata of the public, and, on the contrary, stress the positive aspects.[10]

The anxiety of the OECD Secretariat is not misplaced. There is indeed evidence that people are deeply concerned with the lack of social responsibility and accountability for some of the information technologies already installed and operating. How else to explain the sudden temporary halt in the Reagan administration's proposed policy of allowing individual census data to be passed around from one government agency to another? No guardian of the public's right to know or to its right to information privacy, the general outcry was sufficient to stop for the time being, at least, the administration taking another step in the direction of omnipotent information surveillance and control.[11]

Whether large-scale manifestation of public concern over the direction of the information technology can be expected to continue and deepen, remains to be seen.

In sum, longterm cultural impacts may well overturn the short run economic advantages that are today the motivating force behind the communications "revolution." This should not be viewed, however, with unqualified satisfaction. The cultural impacts may be far from neat and their political expression may be less than rational. Yet if the future is clouded, what does seem clear is that the information age now looming carries little promise of fulfilling what its proponents proclaim: ease, well-being, and humanization.

GROWING SEPARATION OF AMERICAN THINKING
FROM INTERNATIONAL REALITIES

Finally, there is one paradox that overshadows all the others in its long-term implications. It is, actually, the summation, or perhaps, outcome, of those paradoxes already mentioned.

Americans are forever being congratulated by their leaders for being the beneficiaries of the most technologically advanced, complex, expensive, and adaptable communication facilities and processes in the world. This notwithstanding, and this is the paradox, people in the United States may be amongst the globe's least knowledgeable in comprehending the sentiments and changes of recent decades in the international arena.

Despite thousands of daily newspapers, hundreds of magazines, innumerable television channels, omnipresent radio, and instantaneous information delivery systems, Americans are sealed off surprisingly well from divergent, outside (or even domestic) opinion.

This comes not exclusively, but largely, from the vigilant "gate keeping" of private U.S. information controllers, i.e., the big international news agencies' filters, the network news strainers, and the editors of the major newspapers and magazine chains.

It comes as well however, from the privileged material position of an extremely large middle class, as well as a good section of the skilled and professional classes, though often these categories overlap significantly. In each instance, there is a demonstrable inability to recognize, but much less empathize, with a huge, have-not world.

It originates also with the very different experiences of the United States population in the wars of the twentieth century. World War I and World War II, devastated much of Europe and parts of Africa and Asia as well. For the United States, the wars were times of great economic growth and expansion and of corporate and individual enrichment.

For these and other reasons, Americans, enveloped in a rapidly forming information-based economy—saturated with messages and images—remain, unable to comprehend or sympathize with the most elemental and powerful feelings and social movements of this era. Symptomatic, if not typical, of this insensitivity, was the reaction of the President of the United States, when informed that more than a hundred nations protested the invasion of Grenada. Reagan exclaimed this news didn't disturb his breakfast.

The consequences of the already great and still growing divergence between American and world sentiment on fundamental issues of peace and social change, can hardly be overstated. The least that can be said is that it creates a perilous atmosphere for the time ahead.

Efforts to achieve national sovereignty, economic autonomy, and cultural independence are accelerating globally. American reactions to these attempts at changing world power relations are (mis)informed and shaped by an information apparatus almost completely dominated by transnational capital and permeated with its perspectives. It is to be expected, and in fact happens, that most of the struggles for change become subjects of suspicion and hostility in America.

The American people are thrust, ever more frequently, into fateful and tragic positions of opposition to international social movements for human material improvement and individual liberation. They are led also, to assess local disputes that have had ancient origins, as issues of potential danger to American survival.

When the content of the messages and the quality of the news reporting come under scrutiny in international discussions, American representatives of the transnational information apparatus, invoke "freedom of the press" and the U.S. Constitution's First Amendment. Though increasingly regarded with skepticism outside the country, this tactic still serves to persuade Americans, that the world is filled with tyrants seeking to curtail their informational freedom.

At the same time the omission, distortion, and partial representation of global events and popular sentiments, in the American media, assume phenomenal levels.

What may be expected, eventually, from the combination of a misinformed and under-informed people, supporting a government, representative of transnational corporate interests, armed with nuclear weapons of unimaginable destructive capacity? It can only be hoped that the paradoxes that have been described above may succeed in unhinging or overturning some of the dangerous relationships and directions that now prevail.

NOTES TO CHAPTER SIX

1. P. Hetherington, "The Electronic Warning For the Trade Unions," The *Guardian* (England), April 23, 1983, p. 19.

2. B. Newman, "Single-Country Unions of Europe Try to Cope with Multinationals," The *Wall Street Journal,* November 30, 1983, p. 1.

3. Guenter Friedrichs and Adam Schaff, editors, *Micro-Electronics and Society,* Club of Rome report, Mentor, New York, 1983, p. 24.

4. George Shultz, *Chronicle of International Communication,* Vol. IV, No. 8, October, 1983, p. 2.

5. Charles P. Lecht, "The A.T.& T. Strike: Automate or Die," *Computerworld,* August 22, 1983, p. 35.

6. Robert Lindsey, "Unions Press Drive To Enlist High-Technology Workers," The *New York Times,* May 25, 1983.

7. *See,* for example, the study of commercial television's view of labor in, "Television: Voice of Corporate America," The *Machinist,* 1981.

8. Friedrichs and Schaff, *op. cit.,* pp. 32 and 152.

9. Ithiel de Sola Pool, *The Technologies of Freedom,* Cambridge, Harvard, 1983.

10. "Beyond 1984: The Societal Challenge of Information Technology," OECD Secretariat, Proposal for a Conference in 1984. *Document Service,* IIC, October 1983, Vol. III, No. 2.

11. David Burnham, "White House Scraps Plan to Share Census Figures," The *New York Times,* November 24, 1983.

Chapter Seven

The Prospect for Democratic Communication

In the gathering crisis which affects employment, production, and survival itself, the communication process could serve constructive ends if it would be utilized to inform, alert, and mobilize people to the problems that face them, and, if it offered as well, a channel for the presentation and discussion of genuine options.

This, it is clear, is a description of democratic communication. It requires, as one of its indispensable conditions, whatever the size of the political unit, the widest possible public access to and involvement with the means of expression, in both an active and reactive mode. This means popular participation in initiating messages and discussion as well as in responding to messages and discussion. Ideally, this would be effected at the individual level. Minimally, it would guarantee representative expression, subject to continuous popular review and correction.

Is even an approximation of this kind of communication possible in an economy, national or international, that is dominated by huge private companies and combines? Is it even able to exist? If it exists, can it develop?

Historically, the obstacles preventing democratic communication have been physical, technological, and social. Each has been important, alone or in combination, but the ultimate limiting factor has been, and continues to be, social.

Privileged and governing classes, invariably have exercised a tight hold on the communication process. With successive developments in the technology of communication—the emergence of writing and literacy, the invention of printing, the discovery of broadcasting, and most recently, the development of satellites and computers and their linkage—the conditions governing full public access to the means of expression change. The efforts to achieve wider access, therefore, are compelled to seek new forms. And, correspondingly, the means to deny access also change.

The barriers to democratic communication in an industrially developed, high technology market economy are especially complex and often deceptive. The *appearance* is that of information availability and abundance. Indeed, individuals often are unable to escape what amounts to being a continuous informational barrage. Willing or not, most individuals are compelled to live in a message and image-saturated environment. The fact that people are seemingly unrestricted in their communications choices, sometimes leads to equating, mistakenly, the quantity of information with a genuine access to information, and the act of choosing what is offered, with authentic participation in the communication process.

However, the communication process must be seen in the context of prevailing power systems. In the advanced market economies of Western Europe, North America, Japan, and a few other locations, the most salient characteristic is the presence of giant private firms which, in effect, preside over the allocation of resources—in production, employment, investment, income, and profits.

These companies produce the bulk of the goods and services as well as the images and messages that circulate in the society. They employ most of the labor force. They account for the largest share of each nation's foreign transactions. They utilize most of the global communications circuits for their data flows and message transmissions.

In short, the transnational corporation, operating in many different geographical locales internationally, is the dominant force in modern market economies. Its impact is economic, political, and cultural. Its reliance on and influence over communications is both direct and indirect. Altogether it is the primary shaper of the information environment of that part of the world in which it operates.

THE DIRECT IMPACT OF CONGLOMERATES
ON COMMUNICATION

The pattern of private, concentrated ownership of communication facilities is carried furthest in the United States. The press, radio, television, cable, and satellite communications are highly concentrated, capital intensive industries, controlled by huge media chains and conglomerates.

Initially, Western Europe, Canada, Australia, and Japan maintained public (state) systems of broadcasting and telecommunications. Though these remain relatively intact, private broadcasting has become a powerful force in most of these countries, continuing its growth, generally at the expense of the state systems.

Private communications corporations—press and broadcasting—claim that their programming, of necessity, is democratic, because they rely entirely on holding their audience's attention and interest. Without listeners and viewers, they state, correctly, they would quickly lose their advertising revenues.

Though it is certainly true that advertising income depends largely on the size of the audience, it does not follow automatically that commercial programming is the outcome of audiences' preferences or needs. In a commercial system, it is the profitability factor, not the viewer/listener's wants and needs, that receives priority attention.

Audience preferences are often flagrantly disregarded. The determining factor is whether or not it is a *desirable* audience. Desirability is measured by age and income. According to a commercial calculus, old people, poor people, low-income people, and often people of color constitute, in the main, unwanted audiences.

There is a still more important limiting condition to democratic communication in an advanced, industrial market economy. It is the very high cost of establishing a facility for expression. The greater the amount of technology employed in the communication process, the higher the costs of undertaking message production and transmission. As newspapers, radio, TV, and cable are notably high technology industries, the capital required to start up in any of these media is far beyond the means of local groups and public associations, to say nothing of ordinary citizens. It is also beyond most individual holdings of wealth.

Consequently, there has been an accelerating takeover of communication facilities and structures in most developed market economies by large and private media combines. As only the very largest aggregations of capital can enter these fields, the means of communication preponderantly are owned and are at the disposal of giant, conglomerate firms, which are often engaged in a variety of communications and media activities.

By the end of the nineteenth century, observers of the American social scene were writing about the concentration of industrial wealth and media power. Though new industries appeared, the concentration grew more intense throughout the twentieth century. Nowhere is this more evident than in the media industries.

One keen observer of journalistic developments, Ben Bagdikian, finds that:

> Today fifty corporations own most of the output of daily newspapers and most of the sales and audiences in magazines, broadcasting, books and movies ...The fifty men and women [sic] who head these corporations...constitute a new Private Ministry of Information and Culture.

And there is still another side to the media power edifice:

> The concentration of giant media firms that control American public information is troublesome by itself. The interlocking directorates with each other and

with major industries and banks, insurance companies, and investments firms make it more troublesome still.[1]

The opportunity for independent, small-scale expression, though not completely absent, is kept at the fringes and margin of the society. Diversity of expression, therefore, though not entirely eliminated, is severely restricted and subject to arbitrary and capricious checks.

The great cost of acquiring communication facilities in a high technology economy is but one, though the decisive factor in sharply limiting public expression and debate. A second restrictive condition also derives from the private ownership of communications facilities. Accessibility to the media system, in terms of *use,* depends heavily on the message maker's and transmitter's prospective ability to pay. Who can afford to pay for time and space in the media that reach large publics?

It is predictable, once again, that the voices that are seen and heard and the views that are read, are those of the large corporations, employing equally large advertising agencies as their intermediaries. The costs of taking a full page advertisement in a major newspaper is ordinarily far beyond the means of non-corporate groups and individuals.

In some poor countries, where there are insurgency movements, the insurgents secure newspaper space at home and in major capitals by holding hostages generally captured from the transnational executive corps in the country.

This opportunity is not always present, and other means are sought. For example, after the American invasion of Grenada in the Fall of 1983, the Cuban leader, Fidel Castro, felt obligated to respond to the American charge that the Cubans on the island were a menace to U.S. security. Yet for Castro's statement to reach a small, though influential part of the American public, the Cuban government was forced to pay out of its meager foreign exchange holdings the relatively huge cost of buying a full-page of advertising in the *New York Times.*[2] Otherwise, there was absolutely no likelihood that the full text of the Cuban message would have been published or broadcast in the United States.

Thirty-second commercials (advertisements) on American TV, in choice time periods, when there are huge audiences, now may cost upwards of a quarter of a million dollars. It is no wonder that the most prominent national advertisers on U.S. television are the largest corporations. This phenomenon is characteristic also of the media in the less industrialized world. Surveys in less developed countries confirm the domination of national television viewing time by the advertising of the transnational companies.

It may be argued that advertising is merely commercial expression and should not be confused with political and social speech. So it is, but the omnipresence and influence of advertising in the high tech market economies no longer is confined to the limits of marketing commercial products. In these economies, advertising has been extended to politics, politicians, governmental policy, and general socio-economic issues.

The sums now spent on media advertising in elections in the United States, begin to match the expenditures of the largest corporate advertisers for commercial products and services. Local as well as national political contests rely heavily on media sponsorship. Lacking serious constraints on such activity and expenditures, in the United States at least, the major contributors to political campaigns are the big private enterprises and their trade associations, often utilizing a variety of distributional outlets to conceal the magnitude of the sums expended.

Under these circumstances, the political process begins to resemble a contest of contending corporate contributors to competing candidates, all of whom are essentially dependent on the same funding sources. Though much is made of the small, individual contributor and "grass roots" funding, the bulk of the money raised for political campaigning comes from corporate treasuries and goes into the major media treasuries.

Candidates are "sold" to the public, much like soap and automobiles. But the marketing doesn't end there. Issues of public policy, when considered at all, increasingly receive their expression and discussion in thirty-second radio and television commercials. What this does to the democratic process can only be imagined. The public gradually has become accustomed to the notion that any issue, however complex, can be outlined, explained, and evaluated in half a minute. "Issue advertising" such as this is, much like "objective" true and false examinations, compresses difficult questions into binary polarities and unlike the tests, utilizes colorful imagery, accompanied by motion and sometimes music.

Beyond the violence imposed on the process of thought and reflection, the reduction of political debate to media advertisements, further limits its range to the pocketbooks of the big corporations and the transnational companies.

Yet to a very considerable extent, the information and entertainment functions in the United States have been preempted by marketing. Totally dependent on advertising revenues, television, radio, and much of the press, use as much as possible, and always a large portion of their time and space, for marketing messages. Additionally, a substantial part of the programming is conceived and produced for its marketing potential and effectiveness.

Ingeniously, this has been made into a virtue by the defenders of the prevailing informational system. It is claimed that a large number and variety of advertisers reduces the dependence of any one media vehicle on a monopoly advertiser. But while this may be correct, the necessity of *all* the media to defend the *systemic* needs of the corporate order is increased.

What this means is that, while it is imaginable for a newspaper, radio station, or television channel to disregard the pressure of a specific advertiser, it is unimaginable for the basic interests of the overall corporate order to be ignored or put into question. Labor-management conflict, the character of private enterprise, and the foreign policy positions of the corporate-governmental coalition are not areas where the media are going to demonstrate adventurousness.

But beyond the use of advertising to achieve corporate, political, and economic objectives, there is still another, perhaps deeper dimension, which deserves particular attention. This concerns the nature of democracy itself.

The full effects of the preemption of a national communications system for marketing are beyond simple analysis. There is one consequence, however, which is hard to miss. Each marketing message is accompanied, in the same container, so to speak, by another socio-political message. The two are actually inseparable. The first is the exhortation or appeal to buy this or that good or service. The second, embedded deeply in the first, is the assumption that the act of buying is an exercise of individual choice. By extension, the act of buying is a democratic act. In this schema, a supermarket is a democratic citadel, the place where democracy is practiced daily by shoppers in their numerous decisions and choices.

This outlook has its origins in marketing practices in American history. In the early 1900s, for example, a period of heavy immigration into the country, the newcomers were persuaded that consumption constituted the means to achieving Americanization.[3] This has been the corporate-sponsored deep structured message for decades.

Yet once the idea is accepted that consumer choice, itself a highly controlled activity, is indistinguishable from the general democratic process and, in fact, is its fullest embodiment, the basic constituents of genuine democracy can be put aside and disregarded. This thinking is far advanced in the consumer societies and in the United States especially. To be sure, its maintenance requires an economy capable of constant growth. Economic contraction and unemployment undermine acceptance of a democracy of consumption.

ANCILLARY FORMS OF INFORMATION-BASED SOCIAL CONTROLS

The preoccupation with marketing and the emphasis on advertising, which have characterized the United States economy in the twentieth century and which have been extended to or adopted in other market economies at an accelerating pace since the end of the Second World War, have assisted the growth of ancillary communication activities. These have become potentially powerful elements of social control, and in their utilization, instruments for "directing" the democratic process.

As it was essential to determine whether or not the advertising/marketing message was reaching its target—the individual—means were devised to discover, what, in fact, was happening. This, in brief, is the origin of the marketing survey, which evolved into the opinion poll. As the statistical methodology improved, it became possible, with a carefully selected sample of a larger population, to ascertain, a group's attitudes, views, and reactions to what it had seen, heard, or read about. These replies, tabulated, are now regarded as scientific evidence of public opinion. Scientific or not, the results are used by marketeers, politicians, and eventually all the power clusters in the society, most notably the corporations, the government, and the media as well.

The opinion poll is a remarkable achievement. It purports, quite successfully, to be an instrument of democracy, in that it monitors or registers the public's sentiments on whatever may be the issue some group, usually of considerable influence, is concerned with promoting or discouraging.

However, in a stratified society, with sharply differing levels of income, wealth, and power, the opinion poll and survey are more likely to be available to the governors than to the governed. This is so because polls are costly to undertake. Consequently, their practitioners are generally more closely aligned to the command layers of the social system. Thus, the poll, an invention with democratic potential, is utilized for the most part, for public surveillance and social manipulation.

Polls financed by the government, or just as likely by some private organization with a vested interest in the questions being asked, may seek to ascertain the population's sentiments, for example, toward the new information technologies. (Indeed, there are many such instances of this kind of survey and in Chapter 1, a poll undertaken for the British government on this issue is referred to.)

The poll's findings become available to the financial underwriter of the survey. Then the information machine and whatever other instruments that are deemed useful, are set into motion or put at the service of either reshaping the views that have been provided, or, to make policies *appear* to correspond to the sentiments expressed.

Most polls are surveys intended to assist corporations to be as effective as possible in their marketing efforts.

The enormous concentration of capital in private hands that has been achieved in the last forty years, has elevated a few thousand corporations, at most, to national authority and world domination.[4]

Public relations activities for these companies now have become much more than their original limited task of providing flattering images of corporate leaders and their firms. Today, public relations include the presentation, as unobtrusively as possible in all media, of corporate views on political, economic, and cultural questions, couched in reasonable and effective formats. For these activities, too, to be successful, polls are extremely helpful.

And so, in the modern, market economy, not only are the media filled with advertisements and the programming largely determined by corporate sponsors, but an additional communications infrastructure of polling and public relations financed largely by the super corporations, works tirelessly to frame positions, create messages, and elaborate definitions to accord with what the public *believes are its own ideas.*

The machinery for information creation, attitude formation, and definitional authority is vested almost entirely in the private, corporate sector and in those branches of the government most identified with that sector—the military, financial, and foreign policy branches.

THE DIRECT MEDIA

It is evident that corporate conglomerates and transnational companies have little difficulty in getting their voices heard and their views aired. Indeed, it could be argued that they are so successful in doing so that there is hardly any space open for differing perspectives.

Still, the corporate sector is dissatisfied. It claims that it is often maligned in the mass media. It believes social issues are presented unfairly and that television entertainment ridicules and insults business and business people.

Paradoxically, what bothers a good part of the corporate sector, despite its actual monopolistic grip on the information apparatus, is the profit-seeking behavior of part of its own family—the big, private communications combines.

The communications conglomerates make their money by selling their audiences to the advertisers, who are the rest of the corporate community. But to have audiences to sell, there must be programming that catches and holds viewers/listeners. The formula found to accomplish this, often utilizes some kind of social negativism; violence, crime, disaster, menace. The corporation or corporate executive, as obvious repositories of power, are useful ingredients in audience-catching drama. Then, too, even the slightest media attention to corporate responsibility for current social failures—difficult to overlook entirely—arouses resentment in the executive boardrooms.

For these and other reasons, many of the biggest companies, in addition to their continued heavy use of the general media system, are beginning to create, with newly-acquired in-house facilities, their own media messages, without intermediaries. They are building broadcasting studios, creating cable networks, producing television programs, and distributing films and TV cassettes and a huge amount of printed materials.

Direct corporate communications to local, regional, national, and international audiences are already significant. This development contributes further to the all-encompassing effort to fabricate a total corporate information environment in the advanced market societies.

The means by which transnational corporations and super combines are reaching publics, directly with their own productions and indirectly by means of their access to the major communication circuits with advertising, along with their utilization of the polling and public relations industries, are essentially *instrumental*. That is, the message is subject to the deliberate control of the message-maker. It can be prepared with the assurance that it will be transmitted as the sender, the corporation, wants it to be. In short, the communications system is employed and utilized by the corporate sector.

There is yet another means, non-instrumental, for accomplishing the same, corporate objective of a pervasive, favorable to business, informational climate. It is one likely to be more effective in the long run. This is the transformation of basic institutions in ways which affect social outcomes fundamentally. When the transformational process itself is complex and relatively obscure to the general public, its effectiveness is still greater.

The most striking example of this process of deep, structural change and control has been repeatedly touched on in this book. It is the rapidly unfolding process of making information, in its many forms, a saleable good—a commodity. This development, more advanced in the United States than elsewhere, but also appearing in Western Europe and Japan, is the outcome, as has been noted, of several autonomous factors. In no way can it be attributed to a specific, planning center. Actually, the growth of the transnational corporate system has been a powerful contributing force to what is now happening, though it too is influenced by the process in motion.

The great need of transnational enterprise for huge amounts of data to carry on its operations in many different locales is a major spur to this development. Also, the capacity of computer systems to generate, process, store, and disseminate data on an altogether new scale, is another vital element in the movement to commoditize information.

The transformation of public and social information into private, saleable data is well under way, though its consequences have only begun to be considered.[5]

What the longterm social impact will be of turning information into a saleable good, is difficult to predict. One conclusion already is reasonably clear. The commoditization of information constitutes another considerable step toward the consolidation of privatization in individual life and consciousness. It adds further to making what Raymond Williams calls the outlook and practice of "narrow advantage,"[6] a pervasive feature of the social landscape.

Beyond the direct impact on the individual, the commercialization of information further undercuts the public sphere of life and introduces market criteria into new areas of social interaction. This is a fundamental development and deserves emphasis.

If any principle represents the antithesis of the democratic process, it is the market criterion—the ability-to-pay formula. When this standard is applied to the production and dissemination of information, it means that those without or with limited financial capability get little, no, or at best, useless information. Yet doing without information is tantamount to being excluded from the democratic process.

Still, it is this principle that now is being introduced across the informational spectrum—from pay TV, to "deregulated" telephone services, to charges for on-line data bank services, to the disappearance of modestly priced government and academic information.

Information is being supplied to those who can afford it, and, at the front of the line, is the transnational corporation, with its insatiable need for specialized information and processed data.

Besides the inequality of access to information that an ability-to-pay standard imposes, there is another structural effect of even greater longterm significance. The *kind and character* of the information that will be sought, produced, and disseminated will be determined, if market criteria prevail, by the most powerful bidders in the information marketplace—the conglomerates and the transnational companies.

Accordingly, as information more and more assumes a commodity form, the chief beneficiaries of this development will be the large business firms, active in national and international markets, whose resources enable them both to secure the new commodity and, of longer lasting significance, to specify what should be the characteristics of that commodity.

THE PROSPECT AHEAD

What then is the hope for democratic communication when information and information technology are being used, not to promote social ends, but to consolidate and rationalize further, an already conglomeratized, transnational economy? What is the likelihood for participation of people in non-manipulated discourse, about the conditions of their daily lives and well-being and the many-sided crises already upon us? Is anything other than exploitative "crisis management" imaginable? A historical perspective gives grounds for cautious hopes.

It is no consolation to observe that democratic communication has rarely, if ever, existed in its ideal state in any political formation. Yet the long march toward humanization has been in the direction of new voices constantly being added to the dialogue, locally, nationally, and internationally.

At the global level, how else may the emergence of more than one hundred new nations since the end of World War II be interpreted? Is it not a widening of the international forum and the appearance on the world stage of a huge section of hitherto unrepresented humanity? Again, this in no way suggests that the new voices are being given equal weight to the older, still powerful ones. But they are not completely drowned out either.[7]

The Media Conference of the Non-Aligned Nations (NAMEDIA) in New Delhi in December 1983, illustrates the current ambiguities. The conference was ignored in the Western media—not a word appeared about it in the *New York Times,* despite the attendance of scores of world figures at the meeting which was opened with a speech of the Prime Minister of India, Indira Gandhi. Nevertheless, by the very fact of its convocation, the conference represented one more significant effort to broaden the parameters of the information issue and place it high on the international agenda of matters requiring consideration and social change.[8]

Inside national boundaries, groups that have been excluded historically from the general decision-making, also are seeking to be heard. Those excluded because of race, class, or gender are demanding their due. It is realistic to take these still not fully articulated forces into account. Otherwise it would seem that the transnational corporate system had matters all its own way.

The financial strength to fill the mass media and other consciousness-shaping institutions with its views, perspectives, and definitions, and the capability to employ the new information technologies for private ends, confer enormous power on the managers of transnational capital. Yet despite its gigantic concentration of capital, political power, and informational control, there are vulnerabilities in the system that create or allow opportunities for popular expression. And, it is not a trivial matter that for the first time in human development, such expression now possesses a global dimension, which may be expected to broaden and deepen.

Furthermore, this expression in no way can be limited to gaining access to the established media channels. Though this is not minimized as a goal, there will be other forms, some already utilized, others to be discovered, that will change significantly, the contours of the international and domestic informational order.

Popular theatre and video, demonstrations, open skirmishing, and, not to be excluded, insurrections, are forms of communication that are relevant to an age of crisis and change. These may well become typical means of future popular expression in one locale after another. In this connection, the valiant women encamped for months at Greenham Common, outside a United States missile base in England, may, in time, be seen to be a greater communicative force than endless system-maintaining broadcasts from the BBC and similar networks.

The national state too, despite its many contradictions and class aspect, may pose serious challenges to the transnational system of capital.

Transnational corporations must secure the agreement of the nations within which they operate, merely to maintain their vital information flows uninterrupted. This agreement cannot any longer be taken for granted.

Also, within the nation, the greater the processing and fabrication of information, the more suspect it becomes. Already significant numbers of people in many counries regard their information sources with skepticism and even mistrust.

In this situation, space becomes available for local and independent voices, generally without resources, but at least able to keep alive and possibly broaden local networks of alternative imagery and information. In the United States, for example, the epicenter of transnational corporate influence and cultural domination, a lively group of independent film and video workers, broadcasters, visual artists, and print journalists engage in local, and sometimes national efforts. Democratic communication exists albeit restricted and mainly in the social interstices.

There are other factors which sometimes enable wider information flows to circulate. It is useful to take account of the internal rivalries and conflicts which erupt from time to time between corporate power groupings. This is particularly observable in the current era of great technological change and industrial upheaval. Whole industries are disappearing while new ones quickly become powerful. At the same time, the adaptations are nowhere near so rapid in the lives of millions of people. These calamitous conditions are difficult to conceal and still more difficult to overcome in a heavily concentrated, market-directed economy. But they do create receptivities for a different dialogue than that which is promoted and imposed by the transnational power structure.

These divisions sometimes permit peoples' needs to gain a hearing. Especially significant here is the conflict between the media conglomerates' interests and the rest of the corporate system's desire for media reticence and quietude.

Not to be minimized also, are the significant numbers of people in the new professions of the information economy, many of whom seek a human application, if that is possible, of the new technologies.

It is a mistake to view all relatively well-paid professionals as unquestioning supporters and allies of the system which employs them. For some this is likely to be the case, but as Raymond Williams correctly observes, many of these information workers have both the education and the social breathing space to enable them to adopt a distanced, if not critical, stance to the emerging institutional arrangements.[9]

Finally, the anti-domination sentiment that has been a powerful current in much of Central and South America, Africa, and Asia in the 20th century, has by no means been exhausted. It still provides the general atmosphere and context within which the international dialogue—be it economic, political, cultural, or informational—proceeds. And this, too, provides a check of sorts on transnational corporate aims and actions as well as a source for future, democratic initiatives.

In sum, it is a far from finished business. The transnational system and its supporters press to organize a world suitable to maintain their privileged interests. Most of the people and the majority of the nations have different needs to defend and aspirations to follow. In the many collisions ahead, information and communication will be decisive spheres of contested terrain.

NOTES TO CHAPTER SEVEN

1. Ben H. Bagdikian, *The Media Monopoly,* Beacon, Boston, 1983, pp. xvi and 27.

2. "Farewell Address by Commander in Chief Fidel Castro, First Secretary of the Central Committee of the Cuban Communist Party and President of the Council of State and Ministers, in funeral homage to the heroes fallen in unequal combat against Yankee Imperialism in Grenada," Advertisement, The *New York Times,* November 20, 1983, p. 40.

3. Stuart Ewen, *Captains of Consciousness,* New York, McGraw Hill, 1976.

4. According to the 1983 "Fortune 500" listing of the largest industrial corporations in the U.S., these economic behemoths accounted for over $1.6 trillion of sales in 1982.

5. Anita R. Schiller, "Shifting Boundaries in Information," *Library Journal,* Vol. 106, No. 7, April 1, 1981, pp. 705–709; Herbert I. Schiller, *Who Knows: Information in the Age of the Fortune 500,* Norwood, New Jersey, Ablex Publishing Corporation, 1981.

6. Raymond Williams, *Towards 2000,* London, Chatto and Windus, 1983, pp. 187–188.

7. Herbert I. Schiller, "Critical Research In The Information Age," *Journal of Communication,* Vol. 33, No. 3, Summer, 1983, pp. 249–257.

8. Media Conference of the Non-Aligned, New Delhi, December 9–12, 1983. Office of the Secretary General, NAMEDIA.

9. Raymond Williams, *op. cit.*

Name Index

Subject Index